The Coaching Toolkit

The Coaching Toolkit

A Practical Guide for Your School

Shaun Allison and Michael Harbour

SAGE

Los Angeles | London | New Delhi
Singapore | Washington DC

SAGE Publications Ltd
1 Oliver's Yard
55 City Road
London EC1Y 1SP

SAGE Publications Inc.
2455 Teller Road
Thousand Oaks, California 91320

SAGE Publications India Pvt Ltd
B 1/I 1 Mohan Cooperative Industrial Area
Mathura Road
New Delhi 110 044

SAGE Publications Asia-Pacific Pte Ltd
33 Pekin Street #02-01
Far East Square
Singapore 048763

Library of Congress Control Number 2007937710

British Library Cataloguing in Publication data

A catalogue record for this book is available from the British Library

ISBN 978-1-4129-4536-3
ISBN 978-1-4129-4537-0 (pbk)

Typeset by C&M Digitals (P) Ltd, Chennai, India
Printed in Great Britain by CPI Antony Rowe, Chippenham, Wiltshire
Printed on paper from sustainable resources

FSC
Mixed Sources
Product group from well-managed
forests and other controlled sources
Cert no. SGS-COC-2953
www.fsc.org
© 1996 Forest Stewardship Council

Contents

About the authors

Shaun Allison

shaun_allison@hotmail.com

Shaun Allison is Assistant Headteacher at Littlehampton Community School in West Sussex, which is a large 11–19 comprehensive. In this role, he has overall responsibility for the Continuing Professional Development of the staff at the school, as well as the induction of Newly Qualified Teachers. He also works very closely with three local Higher Education Institutions, co-ordinating the school placements of their Initial Teacher Training programmes. His other leadership roles at the school include leading the performance management process and evaluating the impact of whole-school improvement initiatives. Prior to this, he was Head of Science at another large comprehensive school in West Sussex. Under his leadership, the department showed continuous improvement at KS3 and GCSE. Since 2005, Continuing Professional Development at the Littlehampton Community School has developed into an innovative and highly personalised programme, with coaching and sharing best practice at its heart.

Michael Harbour

meharbour@hotmail.com

Michael Harbour is a Consultant Headteacher, who has led two co-educational 13–18 comprehensive schools in the United Kingdom. The first successfully operated a joint sixth form with its neighbours, and developed a collaborative cluster of primary, middle and secondary schools (see *'Collaboration, Competition and Cross-phase Liaison: The North Lowestoft Schools Network'* in *Consorting and Collaborating in the Education Marketplace* (1996) Bridges, D. and Husbands, C. (eds) London: Falmer Press). The second, a school in challenging circumstances, achieved four years of continuous GCSE improvement under Michael's leadership. During his time as a Headteacher, he served on the University of East Anglia's Initial Teacher Training Advisory Panel and was a consultant Head in the Suffolk Headteacher Appraisal Scheme. Since becoming an independent consultant in May 2000, he has supported schools facing challenging circumstances in the United Kingdom and in Dominica and St Lucia in the Windward Isles. He has written a guide to school development planning in conjunction with principals and education officers in Dominica, and helped to introduce peer coaching in schools in the south and north of England. He works closely with teachers, senior teams and education officers to build the capacity for sustained school improvement.

Acknowledgements

We are grateful to many people for their contributions to this book and for their support and inspiration.

We would like to thank Julia Vincent, Sue Bond, Julie Woodward, Ian Boundy, Trevor Pask and colleagues at Bognor Regis Community College, West Sussex, who embraced coaching wholeheartedly and who gave generously of their time to reflect on their experiences. We thank John Morrison for his wise counsel and unfailing belief in his staff's capacity to make a difference.

We are indebted to Jayne Wilson for her commitment and support for the development of coaching at Littlehampton Community School and to her staff who have engaged with the coaching process.

Many thanks to Will Thomas for his clarity, theoretical framework and vision of coaching, and for getting us started.

We would like to thank colleagues at Patcham High School, in particular Paula Sargent for her invaluable suggestions about measuring the impact of coaching, John McKee for his enthusiasm and passion for developing coaching in schools, and Pete Korman for the many conversations that helped to clear the fog.

We are grateful to Bill Whiting, Vicky Whitlock, Austen Hindman, Kerrie Parsons and the staff at Mayfield School, Portsmouth, whose determination and teamwork were inspirational, and to Ian Cox for encouraging all of us to step outside our comfort zone.

Our thanks go to two colleagues in particular in the West Sussex Advisory Service – Lesley Smith for challenging assumptions and for being so clear about how to support the work of coaches, and to Mark Wilson for his grounded approach to whole-staff coaching training.

We are indebted to Katie Morgan for her useful case study, and Tracy Smith and the rest of the teaching staff at Seven Kings High School for their inspirational work on Assessment for Learning.

Our thanks must also go to all those coaches and coachees with whom we have worked in schools and from whom we have learned.

Finally our thanks to Jude Bowen and Amy Jarrold for guiding us through the publication process.

Key to icons

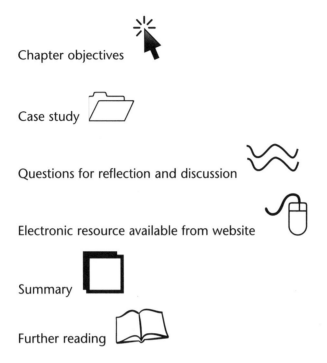

Chapter objectives

Case study

Questions for reflection and discussion

Electronic resource available from website

Summary

Further reading

List of electronic resource materials

Wherever you see the ⌂ icon, downloadable material can be found at www.sagepub.co.uk/allison for use in your setting. A full list of materials follows.

Chapter 1
    Beliefs and principles of coaching
    Beliefs about learning and teaching
    Coaching, counselling and mentoring definitions
    Peer coaching
    The effective coach

Chapter 2
    Coaching helps people to …
    Coaching is based on …
    Skills–motivation matrix
    Why coaching? 1 and 2

Chapter 3
    Record of coaching conversation (FLOW)
    Record of coaching conversation (STRIDE)
    Self-talk and performance success task

Chapter 5
    Coaching prompt cards
    NQT co-coaching – lesson observation review sheet

Chapter 8
    Teaching audit
    Procedures for peer coaching
    CPD staff questionnaire
    Protocol for peer coaching
    Sample coach invite letter

Chapter 9
    The coaching cycle
    Coaching for performance – PowerPoint presentation
    Coaching for performance – training plan
    Coaching for performance – programme
    Request for coaching form

Chapter 10
    Coaching review template
    Job satisfaction chart
    Teacher attitudinal survey
    Whole-school coaching audit
    Student survey

How to use this book

We decided to write this book because we have experienced, in a range of very different schools, the power of coaching to develop teachers' practice. In a 'coaching school', you will hear much conversation about what works effectively in the classroom and you will notice openness about the issues that teachers face, a high degree of self-reflection and a real confidence that teachers will find the solutions to their own challenges. In other words, coaching has the capacity, if properly embedded, to generate enormous positive energy and a 'can do' culture within a staff.

We noticed that, although there are many excellent books on the market about the theory and skills behind coaching, very few writers have paid attention to the practicalities of introducing and embedding coaching in a busy school. We intended to plug this gap, as well as sharing our enthusiasm and experiences with you.

After writing *The Coaching Toolkit*, we have come to one very firm conclusion about using coaching as a staff development tool in schools. That is, there are many ways to go about setting up coaching and some approaches may not fit in with your own ideas or the needs of your institution. This is fine! Bill Whiting, Assistant Headteacher, Mayfield School, Portsmouth, sums this up beautifully, by describing coaching as being like a virus in that it needs to adapt and evolve depending on the conditions and circumstances of the school. Consider the following questions in this context:

- **What is to be the focus for coaching?** The focus of how coaching is used may vary from year to year, or school to school. For example, the whole school may be involved in coaching trios, or coaching may be used to develop teachers in their second year of teaching.

- **What are the school's circumstances?** Schools are clearly very different places, because of the circumstances they find themselves in (special measures, 'coasting', low morale, dynamic, pro-active ...). These differing circumstances will determine how coaching will be used.

- **What is the climate of the school?** In schools with different cultures, coaching could be viewed as:

  o a tool to address failure and weakness

  o Continuing Professional Development (CPD)

  o a tool to celebrate strengths

  o a way of improving practice

  o a way of developing people.

The challenge is finding the right way to do it in *your* school. What have other schools done to establish coaching? What were the practicalities? What were the problems? How did they overcome these problems?

Finding the answers to these questions, based on the real experiences of schools, is not easy. Coaching as a staff development process in schools is relatively new. Schools are still trying it out for themselves – seeing what does and does not work. We have been doing what we tend to do a great deal in education, and that is working in isolation – trying to work through a problem that has probably been experienced and solved by an institution 20 miles up the road. This book provides a means for sharing some of the good practice that schools have developed.

The strategies and resources in the book have all been developed and used by the authors and their colleagues in schools in England. Shaun has worked with Mike in his own school, Littlehampton Community School, to develop coaching with a view to improving the quality of teaching and learning for three years. During this period the school has seen a steady improvement in the examination outcomes of its students. Mike has also worked with leaders in a number of other schools, many of which have been in 'challenging circumstances' requiring swift improvement following an inspection. He has worked with these schools to develop coaching. All of these schools, have made significant improvements and have been successful in addressing the issues raised following their inspection. We have taken the opportunity to reflect on and celebrate their successes in this book.

As coaching develops in a school, some of the things we put into place will work well and serve to move coaching and, as a result, teaching and learning on, whilst other initiatives will not work so well and will be abandoned or further developed. What does happen though is that coaching will evolve and develop a life of its own – again, like a virus!

What is clear, however, is that the skills of coaching are generic. They can be used successfully with children and with adults in schools of all sizes, from small primary to large secondary, in urban and rural settings and in schools with a range of strengths and weaknesses.

How you can use this book in your school

Chapters 1–3 are designed to help the practitioner to clarify what coaching is about and to begin using it as a tool to support the development of learning and teaching.

Chapter 1 deals with the question, what is coaching? It then goes on to look at the differences and similarities between mentoring and coaching. It also explores some of the models that are available for the structuring of coaching conversations and finally looks at the skills needed to become an effective coach.

Chapter 2 explores why coaching is a powerful developmental tool for teachers and looks at the impact of coaching on teaching and learning compared to other professional development activities.

We hope that Chapter 3 will be especially useful to teachers who are relatively new to coaching. Here we suggest:

- ways of practising coaching skills before 'going live' with coachees

- how to establish the ground rules for coaching conversations

- how to conduct coaching conversations

- how to give feedback on an observed lesson in coaching mode.

Chapters 4–6 examine the use of coaching for different purposes and will be of value to practising coaches and school leaders alike.

In Chapter 4 we define specialist coaching and consider how school leaders can use it to address specific developmental priorities within their school. We also look at how coaching can play an integral role in performance management and consider the wider issues of collaborative working within schools.

Chapter 5 explores how co-coaching can be used to develop Newly Qualified Teachers (NQTs) and teachers in their second year of teaching.

In Chapter 6 we look at group coaching and suggest that knowledge of how adults learn is important in the setting up of coaching groups. We then go on to look at how different groups of staff could use coaching as a development tool for a variety of purposes.

Chapter 7 shows how coaching can rapidly develop and can have a significant impact on teaching and learning, despite challenging circumstances. The case studies illustrate best practice in the development of coaching trios; the use of lead teachers to drive the coaching process; how to support the work of a coaching team; how coaching can be used to support the work of one department; how to measure the impact of coaching. The lessons learned in the two schools can be applied in a range of different school contexts.

Chapters 8–10 are of particular interest to school leaders and deal with many of the organisational issues associated with setting up, sustaining and measuring the impact of coaching in schools.

In Chapter 8 we suggest how to carry out a whole-school CPD audit, how to identify and train potential coaches and how to establish whole-school coaching protocols.

Chapter 9 deals with some of the issues that arise as coaching develops in the school. It also considers how to promote the idea of coaching to the whole school, how to identify the needs of different coachees and match them with a coach and how to meet the development needs of coaches.

In Chapter 10 we explore the issues around measuring the impact of coaching in schools and suggest ways in which it can be done. Finally, we look at how to audit the development of coaching.

Whenever you see the downloadable resources icon   materials are available from
the website to support this book and can be used and adapted for your context.

It is hoped that this book will provide school leaders at all levels, including teachers who are leaders in their classrooms, with something that we couldn't find when
trying to establish coaching in a range of different schools – a practical, hands-on
guide to developing coaching at your school.

We do not claim to be experts in this area; there are many more colleagues working in the field of performance coaching who have a far greater knowledge base of
the theory of coaching. However, we both have hands-on experience of setting up
coaching in a range of secondary schools. We have also been fortunate enough to
have worked with a number of very talented teachers and coaches, who have been
keen to share their expertise and experiences of coaching. We thank them.

1

What is coaching?

> **In this chapter we will look at:**
> - **what coaching is**
> - **the differences between mentoring and coaching**
> - **a variety of coaching models that can be used in schools**
> - **what makes a good coach.**

Good teachers can be developed, providing they are working in a supportive and positive environment where it is okay to try things out, make mistakes and then further refine their ideas. They also need to be able to reflect on the issues that are important to them with an encouraging colleague, who will listen and ask key questions to help them find their solution – not the 'this is the way I do it, so you should do the same' approach. This, in our view, is the essence of coaching.

In the sixteenth century, the English language defined 'coach' as a carriage, a vehicle for conveying valuable people from where they are, to where they want to be. It is worth holding on to this definition when talking about coaching in schools. The staff are the most valuable resource that a school has. They are the people that make the difference to the young learners that come to our schools. We therefore have a duty to help and support each other, to become the best teachers that we can possibly be. Coaching is a vehicle to do this.

> *'The good news is that as a teacher you make a difference. The bad news is that as a teacher you make a difference.'* (Sir John Jones, speaking at the Accelerated Learning in Training and Education (ALITE) conference, 2006)

Teachers are often all too aware of when things are not going well and how they would like things to be – what is often called their 'preferred future state'. What we often struggle with is how to get there. What do I need to change? What can I do differently? Why is it not working? A coach is a trusted colleague who asks the right questions to help you find your own way to your preferred future state.

It is important to recognise that this is not new, not rocket science, nor is it a panacea. Teachers in schools have been supporting each other in this way for many years. The skills of a good coach will be examined later on but, put simply, they are listening, questioning, clarifying and reflecting. To coach successfully in schools, you do not need vast amounts of training or a certificate – you just need to have experienced it and to have reflected on its value. We are not talking about life coaching here nor about counselling, which are two very different things that should most definitely be left to the experts. It is the simplicity of coaching in a school setting that makes it such a useful, universal and powerful developmental tool. However, it is only a tool – a very powerful one – but one of many that should be stored and used in the professional development toolbox. It would be naïve to believe that coaching is the 'teacher's cure-all'.

When examining definitions of 'coaching' it is clear that there are common threads running through all of them. They all suggest that coaching is a professional relationship, based on trust, where the coach helps the coachee to find the solutions to their problems for themselves. Coaching is not about telling, it is about asking and focusing. This is what separates mentoring from coaching. A mentor is often used when somebody is either new to the profession, for example a teacher in training or NQT, or is new to a particular role in the school. The mentor will have more experience than the person being mentored in that particular role, and so passes on their knowledge and skills. With coaching, the approach is different. It is more concerned with drawing out the solutions to a problem, by effective questioning and listening. It is non-hierarchical and does not depend on any expert/subject specific knowledge. In fact, one of the most successful coaching relationships that we have seen involved a NQT coaching an experienced teacher of nearly 30 years on how to effectively incorporate information and communication technology (ICT) into her lessons.

> ### 📁 Case study: Sarah and Jan
>
> Jan was a physical education (PE) teacher with nearly 30 years of teaching experience. She was a good and well-respected teacher, who had recently started teaching English to Year 7. Sarah was an English NQT. Jan had identified that she wanted to make her lessons more engaging by using her newly acquired interactive whiteboard. She didn't want to attend a course on this but had been impressed with some of the lessons of her colleague, Sarah, who taught next door. Following a school training day on coaching, Jan asked Sarah if she could coach her. The two soon struck up a highly effective coaching relationship, which involved three coaching sessions and two lesson observations – each observing the other. Jan described how she felt at the end of the process: 'Sarah helped me to clarify exactly what I wanted to achieve, and the steps I had to take to get there. As a result, I now feel confident using my interactive whiteboard and have achieved my goal – to deliver more interesting and engaging lessons'.

It is worth acknowledging that this relationship was an unusual one – in terms of the difference in experience of the coach and the coachee. However, it does demonstrate the non-hierarchical nature of coaching.

Many of the skills of good mentoring and good coaching overlap – and often a blended approach of the two is most effective. When supporting a colleague, it is important not to be constrained by the labels of 'coaching' and 'mentoring'. By this we mean that, if during a coaching conversation it becomes clear that no amount of

Continuum support and development	
Mentoring	Coaching
Instructing	Questioning
Input	Drawing out
Hierarchical	Non-hierarchical
Assumes subject-specific expertise	Subject-specific expertise not required

Figure 1.1   Continuum of support and development

questioning, reflecting, listening or clarifying is going to move the person on, then sometimes you need to slip into mentoring mode and make a suggestion. There is nothing wrong with this, although we suggest that it may be helpful to be explicit when adopting a different stance by, for example, asking permission of your colleague – 'Would it be all right if I were to suggest a possible course of action here?'. Alternatively, the coach may be able to tap into the coachee's preferred future and ask the coachee to visualise a possibility – 'What would it look like if you were to …?'.

Mentoring and coaching should be seen as a continuum in terms of supporting and developing teachers.

This blended approach is often evident when mentoring NQTs. When the NQTs are starting out, it is very much a mentoring relationship. You will be imparting your knowledge and skills to the NQTs, so that they can develop as teachers. As the mentees become more confident and competent, the balance between mentoring and coaching shifts further along the continuum towards coaching.

One other important difference between coaching and mentoring is that of making judgements. Often a mentor has to make a judgement about the standard reached by the person being mentored, for example has he or she met the qualified teacher status (QTS) standards or the induction standards? This will result in quite a different relationship from that between coach and coachee, where it is very important not to be judgemental.

So, what are the skills that make a good coach? It is widely agreed that there are four:

- **listening**

- asking open **questions**

- **clarifying** points

- encouraging **reflection.**

Examples of these will be discussed later. Coaches also need to be good at:

- building rapport – using posture, gestures, eye contact and so on

- adopting a non-judgemental view of others

- challenging beliefs – a good coach must be willing to have difficult conversations

- seeing the big picture – this is at the heart of good coaching. Ask the question – 'So what do you want to achieve? What do you want to be better?'

- summing up – this helps to keep the conversation focused and on track. For example, 'So, what you're saying is you want to improve ...'

- encouraging others to agree on actions – an essential part of the coaching process is committing people to action. For example, 'So, following our discussion you are going to ...'

- acknowledging that they don't have all the answers – this is fine. The role of the coach is to elicit the answers from the coachee

- respecting confidentiality

- developing a mutual trust and respect

- adopting a solutions focus – once the issues have been uncovered, don't allow the conversation to descend into a spiral of negativity. Direct the coachee onto what they are going to do about it

- holding a strong belief that colleagues have the capacity to learn, develop and change.

They also have the following qualities:

- curiosity
- optimism
- honesty
- trustworthiness

- patience
- consistency
- flexibility
- creativity

- confidence
- approachability
- professionalism
- openness

The importance of questioning in coaching

It should be clear by now that the principles behind coaching are straightforward. It is fundamentally about using questioning and listening skills to help coachees to resolve their own issues. However, there are a number of different coaching models that can be used to achieve this (see below). These models provide a framework for the coaching conversation – the dialogue between the coach and the coachee.

With all of these models, if a coaching conversation is to be successful, the coach will be required to use a range of different questioning strategies.

Clarifying questions

The purpose of this type of questioning is to clarify the issue – to get to the nuts and bolts, and so clear the way for deeper thinking. For example:

- 'Tell me more about ...'

- 'What aspect of this do you want to discuss today?'

- 'When have you had success in this area? Tell me more about that'

- 'I am interested to hear about ...'

- 'You say that your starters are too long. Is that always the case?'

- 'What makes you think that this is an issue?'

Reflective questions

Reflective questions encourage the coachee to think about and reflect on their practice. For example:

- 'What do you want your starter activities to achieve?'

- 'What factors do you take into account when planning your lessons?'

- 'What did you want the students to learn today?'

- 'What would have to change in order for ...?'

- 'What do you wish ...?'

- 'What's another way you might ...?'

- 'What would it look like if ...?'

- 'What do you think would happen if ...?'

- 'How was ... different from ...?'

- 'What sort of an impact do you think ...?'

- 'What might you see happening in your classroom if ...?'

- 'What is your hunch about ...?'

- 'What was your intention when ...?'

Summarising questions

These are useful when the conversation has drifted away and you want to get the focus back. They are also useful to check that you have listened effectively and that the coachee has communicated accurately. For example:

- 'So, to summarise, you say that the following factors are resulting in your starters taking too long ... is that right?'

- 'So, you are saying the key issue is ...'

- 'So, in order to achieve this, you say that you are going to ...'

Outcome questions

Towards the end of the coaching conversation, you will want the coachee to commit to action. The following questions may help:

- 'What is your first step to achieve this?'

- 'What will you do next?'

- 'What support do you need?'

- 'On a scale of 1 to 10, how compelled are you to do this?'

- 'What will it look like, when you are successful?'

It should be noted that the majority of these are open questions. An open question directs the respondent away from a 'yes' or 'no' answer, but towards a longer and more reflective response. Open questions will usually start with what, how and describe, for example, what happened when you tried that strategy with this class? What leads you to think that it will not work? How would you do that differently next time? Can you describe one strategy you have used that has been successful? It is helpful to avoid 'why?' questions as they may sound too critical. (See Chapter 3 Getting Started – The 'shape' of the conversation).

Listening: the most difficult skill!

When coaching we must work hard to focus on our coachee's words, tone of voice, body language and what is not being said, as well as what is, in order to ask the right question at the right time. We must not anticipate or construct possible solutions for our colleague – that is not our job. So, our listening skills need to be acute and, of course, they will develop with practice.

It is useful to recognise that we listen at three different levels.

Internal listening

Here we are listening to the self-talk inside our heads. Our colleague's comments can, and often do, prompt thoughts of our own. How many times, whilst in conversation, have you found yourself thinking, 'That's just what happened to me the other day … ' or 'I felt exactly the same when …'? Such internal listening acts as 'interference' and prevents the coach from giving the client his or her undivided attention. With practice, coaches learn to filter out the interference and are able to listen actively.

Active listening

This occurs when the coach is paying full attention to the coachee's words, tone of voice, images and figures of speech. Then the coach is able to ask those (usually open-ended) questions, as discussed above, that help the coachee to move towards a solution. Moreover, by focusing all of his or her attention on the coachee, the coach is motivating the coachee. There is, after all, something very special about *really* being listened to in the hectic world of a busy school! This is likely to be very important for the self-esteem and confidence of the coachees, especially if he or she is, as we say, 'in a bad place'.

Intuitive listening

When you are really tuned in as a coach, you begin to learn the thought patterns of your colleague, detect areas that are left unsaid and sense the feelings that lie under the surface of the conversation. You are beginning to listen *intuitively* and this may lead you to ask questions that will help the coachee to explore important and challenging aspects of issues. Such questions as, 'What are your feelings about ...?' or 'Is it significant that you haven't mentioned ...?' may be helpful here.

Finally, before we move on to consider different coaching models, it is important to urge the coach to allow thinking time and to resist shattering the silence with yet another question! When the coachee is in important territory, he or she often needs a lengthy pause in which to explore and formulate thoughts and feelings and to summon up the courage before saying anything. Have the confidence to hold the silence. Be attentive and encouraging, but don't speak!

Coaching models

The acronyms that accompany the following coaching models provide prompts for the different stages of the coaching conversation. This section will examine a range of these models and discuss the differences between them.

STRIDE model

This model has been developed by Will Thomas, author of two very useful books: *Coaching Solutions: Practical Ways to Improve Performance in Education* (Thomas and Smith, 2004) and *Coaching Solutions: Resource Book* (Thomas, 2005). These are two books that we strongly recommend for anybody wishing to explore the skills of coaching in more detail. The STRIDE model is summarised as follows:

- **S**trengths: Affirm the positive throughout and draw attention to their strengths.
- **T**arget: What do you want to achieve as a result of this process?
- **R**eality: What is the current situation like now and what obstacles are there to achieving your goals?
- **I**deas: What could you do to address the situation?
- **D**ecision: What are you going to do? What are the next steps?
- **E**valuation: Check the decision: How committed are you to doing this? Over time: What progress have you made towards meeting these targets?

The essential aspect of the STRIDE model is that it really celebrates the strengths of the coachee so the whole process becomes a very positive experience. However, it does encourage the coachee to consider what obstacles there may be, which could prevent them from reaching their target, but they also have to consider how they could overcome these obstacles. The job of the coach is to keep asking open-ended questions to help the coachee to move towards a solution.

FLOW model

The FLOW model is explained in Powell et al. (2001).

- **F**ind the challenge: What is the issue that you need to address?
- **L**ook at reality: What are things like now?
- **O**pen possibilities: What could you do about it?
- **W**in commitment: What are you going to do and when?

There are clear similarities between the STRIDE and FLOW models. One of the key differences is that the STRIDE model starts by looking at the coachee's preferred future, whereas the FLOW model starts by talking about the challenge, that is, What is it that you want to address? From this starting point will then come the discussion about what the targets are. Both models emphasise the need to look at what the reality is now. This is important, as it will open up a dialogue about what the obstacles or blocks are which are stopping the coachee from making progress. Only once these are brought to the fore can the issue really start to be addressed. It is surprising how often this is the key part of a coaching session and that by just seeing the situation clearly (rather than what was thought or imagined to be the situation), the resolution often becomes obvious and straightforward. Lastly, the STRIDE model encourages the coachee to evaluate both the appropriateness of the target and the progress towards it over time.

GROW model

The GROW model is one of the best known and most widely used coaching models, both within and outside education. It provides a simple yet powerful framework for navigating a route through a problem, as well as providing a means of finding your way when lost. It is described in a number of coaching books, including John Whitmore's excellent book, *Coaching for Performance* (2002).

- **Goal:**   What is the outcome to be achieved? The goal should be as specific as possible and it must be possible to measure whether it has been achieved. So, having identified the goal, questions like 'How will you know that you have achieved that goal?' are useful.
- **Reality:**   What are things like now? What is stopping you from getting there?

(Continued)

(Continued)

- **Options:**   What options do you have to help you get there?
- **Wrap up:**   This is the What, Where, Why, When and How part of the process. At this stage, having explored all of the options, the coachee makes a commitment to action.

The attraction of the GROW model is its simplicity. A useful metaphor for GROW is a map: once you know where you are going (the goal) and where you are (current reality), you can explore possible ways of making the journey (options) and choose the best route.

OUTCOMES model

The OUTCOMES coaching model has been developed by Allan MacKintosh, of PMC Scotland (www.pmcscotland.com). It was designed for managers and sales managers to use, but it is clear to see how it could be adapted for teachers.

- **O**   What are the employees' specific Objectives?
- **U**   Understand the exact reasons why they want to achieve these objectives.
- **T**   Take stock of where they are at present in relation to each objective.
- **C**   Clarify the gap that they have to fill.
- **O**   What Options do they have in order to fill the gap?
- **M**   Motivate to Action.
- **E**   Offer continual Encouragement and Energy.
- **S**   Clarify what Support is needed to ensure actions are carried out.

It is suggested that this in-depth approach to coaching will enable an increase in the coachee's understanding of the issue, which will result in motivation to change and then commitment to action. Although this model needs a disciplined approach to coaching, it is a model that, when used effectively, has been shown to motivate and produce results for both coach and coachee.

CLEAR model

The CLEAR model was developed by Peter Hawkins and is discussed in *Coaching, Mentoring and Organizational Consultancy: Supervision and Development* (Hawkins and Smith, 2006).

- **Contracting:**   Opening the discussion, setting the scope, establishing the desired outcomes and agreeing the ground rules.

(Continued)

(Continued)

- **L**istening: Using active listening and catalytic interventions, the coach helps the coachee to develop an understanding of the situation and generate personal insight.

- **E**xploring: (1) Helping the coachee to understand the personal impact the situation is having on the self. (2) Challenging the coachee to think through possibilities for future action in resolving the situation.

- **A**ction: Supporting the coachee in choosing a way forward and deciding the next step.

- **R**eview: Closing the intervention, reinforcing ground covered, decisions made and value added. The coach also encourages feedback from the client on what was helpful about the coaching process, what was difficult and what she or he would like to be different in future coaching sessions.

The CLEAR model has a number of differences from the other models. It starts by discussing the 'contract'. This allows the ground rules to be set, so the coachee has the opportunity to discuss how he or she would like to be coached. There is then a big emphasis on listening – a key component of coaching. When we are being listened to we feel valued, when we feel valued our self-confidence rises and we are more likely to commit to change. The review stage is also important, as it not only reviews the outcome of the coaching session but also reviews the effectiveness of the process. This is important. We should not just assume that the session has been effective, particularly if there is going to be a further session. We should discuss how useful the session was, and how we could make it even more useful next time.

OSKAR model

This model has been developed by Paul Z. Jackson and Mark McKergow at Solutions Focus and is discussed in *The Solutions Focus: Making Coaching and Change SIMPLE* (2007).

The whole principle of this model is not to look at the problem, as this very rarely yields any solutions, but instead to look at what works well and to do more of this and less of what does not work well.

- **O**utcome: What is the objective of this coaching? What do you want to achieve today?

- **S**caling: On a scale of 0 to 10, with 0 representing the worst it has ever been and 10 the preferred future, where would you put the situation today? You are at n now; what did you do to get this far? How would you know you had got to n+1?

- **K**now-how and resources: What helps you perform at n on the scale, rather than 0? When does the outcome already happen for you – even a little bit? What did you do to make that happen? How did you do that?

- **A**ffirm and action: What's already going well? What is the next small step? You are at n now; what would it take to get you to n+1?

(Continued)

(Continued)

- **Review:**   What's better? What did you do that made the change happen? What effects have the changes had? What do you think will change next?

The positive nature of this approach, coupled to the idea of scaling, makes it an attractive model. This somehow makes the issue more tangible. This approach is similar to the STRIDE model in that it really focuses on the strengths of the coachees, and encourages them to consider how they could use these strengths to address any issues that they may have.

HILDA model

One of the best bits of advice regarding coaching was also one of the simplest. It followed a discussion with a colleague about the importance of not getting too hung up on following a script when it comes to coaching. We felt that it should be a natural and flowing dialogue between two professionals and the coach should not have to constantly refer to a bank of questions, whilst engaged in coaching. This is most off-putting for the coachee and does not help to create the informal and relaxed atmosphere required for coaching. With this in mind, it was suggested that the best type of person to become a coach is a nosey person! Someone who will quite naturally ask question after question in order to find out what they want – and in doing so, will also help the coachee to find out. This simplicity seemed most appealing. Some readers might remember a character called Hilda Ogden – the archetypal nosey neighbour – in *Coronation Street* (a long-running television soap, based in the north of England). What a fantastic coach she could have made, with her continuous probing and incisive questioning. This led us to consider an alternative, simple model for coaching – the HILDA model.

- **Highlight the issue:**   What do the coachees want to address? What do they want to be different and how?

- **Identify the strengths:**   What do they already do well? How can these skills and attributes be used to address the particular issues?

- **Look at the possibilities:**   In an ideal world, with no obstacles, what could they do to address the issues? What is getting in the way of doing this? How could these obstacles be overcome? What have they already tried? What worked and what didn't?

- **Decide and commit to action:**   What are they going to do to address the issues? When are they going to do it? How are they going to do it?

- **Analyse and evaluate the impact:**   How will they know if they have been successful? What will it look like?

Although in its early days, we have used this model in schools with an encouraging degree of success. Its simplicity makes the key stages easy to remember, within the framework of a constant reminder to ask open questions throughout each of the stages.

Questions for reflection and discussion

- Who among your colleagues possesses the qualities of a good coach?
- With whom in your school could you explore ideas about coaching?
- Who might be interested in developing coaching in your school?
- What do you think the pros and cons of the different models we have looked at might be in your own school?

 Summary

- The principles of coaching are consistent throughout these models. What varies is the way in which each of the models approaches coaching. You may, of course, wish to devise your own, based on the best bits of all of the models described above. The advantage of doing this, in collaboration with a range of colleagues from within your school, is that the people using the model will feel a sense of ownership over the approach.

- It is very easy to get bogged down with the theory of coaching – what is right and what is wrong. A coaching conversation should never become a scripted event, so whichever model you decide to use, do so carefully. It would be very off-putting for a coachee to be faced by a coach with a clipboard and a list of questions. It should be a natural dialogue, involving a great deal of listening by the coach and open questioning, aimed at helping the coachee to find a solution.

Electronic resources

Go to www.sagepub.co.uk/allison for electronic resources for this chapter

Beliefs and principles of coaching

Beliefs about learning and teaching

Coaching, counselling and mentoring definitions

Peer coaching

The effective coach

Further reading

Jackson, P. Z. and McKergow, M. (2007) *The Solutions Focus: Making Coaching and Change SIMPLE* (2nd edn). Nicholas Brealey Publishing.

Powell, G., Chambers, M. and Baxter, G. (2001) *Pathways to Coaching*. Bristol: TLO.

Thomas, W. (2005) *Coaching Solutions: Resource Book.* Stafford: Network Educational Press.

Thomas, W. and Smith, A. (2004) *Coaching Solutions: Practical Ways to Improve Performance in Education.* Stafford: Network Educational Press.

Whitmore, J. (2002) *Coaching for Performance.* London: Nicholas Brealey Publishing.

Useful websites

www.thesolutionsfocus.com

www.coachingnetwork.org.uk

www.curee-paccts.com/index.jsp

Why coaching?

> **In this chapter we will look at:**
>
> - why coaching is a powerful developmental tool for teachers
> - the impact of coaching compared with other professional development activities.

Coaching, as a performance-enhancing tool, has its roots very much in the business world. There, if something is not working, or not getting the required results, it is changed rapidly – and often coaching is the tool for that change. Whilst we would not subscribe to the fact that schools should be run and led like or by businesses, there is something to be learned from this approach. There is a tendency, when things are not going well for us, to view the problems as being outside of our control. To illustrate this from a teaching point of view, if students are not as focused or as engaged as we might wish and as a result not making sufficient progress, then we have a choice of action. We can either change our practice to adapt to the situation and hopefully improve things, or carry on regardless, thinking that the problems are not connected to our practice and that something outside of our control might eventually change and address the situation.

This is where coaching comes in. Coaching is a tool that encourages teachers to look at their practice and make changes. Coaching is able to achieve this because of the fact that the person telling the coachee how to change is not an advisor, consultant, leader from within the school or some other expert – it is themselves. The coachees are setting the agenda – they determine the issue they want to look at, they come up with the solutions and they determine the timeline for the action they decide to take. Once people have decided for themselves to commit to action, this is a great motivator for achieving their own goals. All the coach is doing is facilitating this process and witnessing the commitment and the change. Do not underestimate the power of the witness. People are far more likely to act if they have set their own targets in the presence of a colleague, the coach, who is genuinely interested in them.

> **Question for reflection and discussion**
>
> To what extent are the staff within your institution willing and able to find their own solutions, when things are not going well?

Julian Rotter (1954) came up with the idea of 'locus of control'. In very simple terms, this is concerned with an individual's perception of the main causes of events in life. Somebody with an 'external locus of control' will feel that their behaviour is guided by fate and luck or other external circumstances. What happens to them is beyond their control. On the other hand, somebody with an 'internal locus of control' will feel that their behaviour is guided by personal decisions and efforts. They are responsible for what happens in their life, and so their actions have a direct effect on their future. A teacher with an external locus of control may view the behaviour of the students as nothing to do with himself or herself – it is all to do with other factors – so there is no need to do anything differently as it will have no effect on the students' behaviour. Following a bad lesson, this teacher may blame the students, the weather, the fact that the bulb on the overhead projector went, the previous lesson that the students had – in fact, anything but themselves. On the other hand, the teacher with an internal locus of control will view the situation differently. Their thought process, following a bad lesson, would be more along the lines of: That didn't go too well – what did I do that didn't work? What could I do next time to make it better?

Coaching can help colleagues to see the link between their actions – in terms of relationships with students, teaching strategies, body language – and the learning, engagement and progress of students. This awareness will then start to shift them from an external to an internal locus of control.

Having introduced coaching, we examined the advantages of having a staff with an internal locus of control achieved through coaching. Following the initial introduction of coaching we had about a dozen coaching pairs set up. After these pairs had been through a coaching cycle, we asked the coachees if they could very simply jot down their thoughts about the process.

This provided us with evidence of the following traits that were developing amongst staff who had been involved in the coaching process:

- **Self-sufficiency**   Staff who can solve their own problems become far more self-sufficient. This is an effective way of working. Instead of problems lingering, becoming worse and then having a bigger negative impact on the students' learning, simply because they are not dealt with (because nobody knows how to), they can be dealt with and addressed quickly and effectively. This minimises the impact that issues have on the learning of the students.

  'The coach I worked with was really supportive. They helped me to work through the issue myself and find a solution. And it worked! As a result, I felt more confident to tackle issues on my own. Really good, thanks very much!' (Maths teacher, five years' experience)

- **Self-esteem**   Staff who feel that they are listened to, but who can deal with their own issues, feel confident. Good teaching and learning is all about confidence. Furthermore, the more confident staff feel, the better equipped they will be to support and develop their peers.

  'The best CPD I have had in the last three years. Brilliant!' (German teacher, three years' experience)

- **Efficiency**   Working in this way enables individuals, groups and the whole school to get to the nub of the problem quickly, to deal with it and move on. The process enables staff to avoid getting distracted by other things that have nothing to do with the real issue – which often wastes a great deal of time in school meetings. However, for this to happen, there needs to be a no-blame culture throughout the school so that people feel safe about discussing the issues they may have.

> *'I took the ideas on board that I discussed with my coach, used them with my classes and as a result felt more confident, organised and generally happier about how the first meetings with my classes went. It has had a knock on effect throughout the year with most of my classes'.* (Science teacher, three years' experience)

- **Team work**   Coaching helps to foster a great team spirit. Why? Because you don't have to be an expert in the issue to coach somebody to help them resolve the issue. This means that everybody has something to offer and so everyone feels valued. Imagine working in a school like that!

> *'Great to see the issue from another angle and come up with a solution … together'.* (Science teacher, two years' experience)

- **A dialogue about pedagogy**   Experience has shown us that as a school goes down the path of coaching, teachers within the school begin to have more of an open dialogue about pedagogy. This is when coaching becomes highly effective.

This process of reflecting on the coaching that had taken place was encouraging as it confirmed what we thought – that coaching has the potential to help support and develop the teaching staff. Although we did note that some of the conversations had perhaps involved mentoring as some coaches had offered their ideas. We say 'potential' because, although we knew that the staff had enjoyed being coached and that their perception of the process was that it was useful, we had not yet measured its impact. Had the coaching really had a significant impact on the learning of the students? This is a topic that we deal with in a later chapter. Nonetheless, if any whole school initiative is to succeed, it needs to have the support and affirmation of the staff.

Coaching vs other CPD activities

 Question for reflection and discussion

What does CPD mean to the staff in your institution? What opportunities for a range of CPD activities does your school provide for the staff?

In recent years, there has been a shift of emphasis towards CPD in school. This has seen staff taking far more responsibility for their own CPD, with schools providing a range of developmental activities for them to engage in. In the forward-thinking school, CPD is less about staff training days and training courses and more about a process of ongoing, collaborative professional learning – where professionals support and learn from each other.

In her book, *The CPD Coordinator's Toolkit*, Sue Kelly describes CPD as: 'any activity which enhances the quality of teaching and learning within the school. It should develop the school and the individual and impact directly on what goes on in the classroom'. (2007: 12) When talking about challenges facing CPD coordinators, she says: 'it is through our work and our vision of what constitutes creative and dynamic CPD practices that we can transform the learning culture in our schools' (2007: 1).

We would argue strongly that coaching meets the goals expressed in both of these statements. It is certainly a strong driver for developing the quality of teaching and learning, as well as establishing a learning culture amongst the staff. A school that invests in coaching will be rewarded with contagious professionalism amongst its staff. Bruce Joyce and Beverley Showers (2002) concluded from a study working with teachers in North America that coaching had a dramatic impact on the transfer and application of new learning. In fact, this application of new learning was significantly higher when acquired through coaching than by other training methods.

The study looked at a range of teacher developmental activities such as:

- lectures on new teaching strategies, during external courses or workshops

- demonstrations of new teaching strategies by 'expert' teachers within the workshop

- practising these new strategies with colleagues attending the workshop

- feedback from the 'expert' teacher or course organiser

- working with a coach on these new strategies in the workplace.

Joyce and Showers then examined how each of these activities impacted on the acquisition of knowledge and skills, and whether they resulted in new strategies being applied to classroom practice. The research found that, while lecturing teachers improved their knowledge of new teaching strategies, it did very little to develop their skills or classroom practice. Seeing the new strategy demonstrated improved skills acquisition slightly, but still did not translate to a change in classroom practice. Skills acquisition did improve when the teacher practised the new strategies in the workshop, but this still did not result in any long-term change in practice. In fact the only way that a significant change was seen in skills/knowledge acquisition and classroom application was when the teachers worked with a coach on the new strategy – in the workplace.

In our experience, this certainly holds true. Until recently, a vast amount of the CPD budget at most schools has probably been spent on sending colleagues on external training courses. They would then return armed with a folder and perhaps a nice pen. However, the impact of the training in terms of changing their teaching strategies was often difficult to see in the classroom. Similarly, any newly acquired skills were not shared amongst colleagues. This seems to be a very expensive and ineffective use of school resources. Unfortunately, staff do not always feel the same way. Unless they have sat in a basement function room of a hotel and had a substantial buffet at lunchtime, they do not feel that they have had proper CPD. This requires a shift of culture and thinking. The range of CPD activities available to staff, including coaching, needs to be sold to staff.

Before we started down the path of coaching, the other two main forms of CPD that staff embarked on, apart from going on external courses, were mentoring and following an MA (Education) programme. It could be argued that both of these are more valid CPD activities, in terms of long-term impact, than external courses. Mentoring, as already discussed, overlaps with coaching, but its uses are limited to colleagues who are either new to teaching or new to a role. Although following an MA course certainly encourages colleagues to think and reflect on their work in school, the extent to which classroom practice changes as a result can be variable. However, while these two activities serve a purpose, we still do not think that they have such a long-term impact on transforming teaching and learning as coaching does.

 Summary

As learning institutions, schools have an obligation to provide a range of opportunities for their staff to engage in professional learning. Coaching facilitates this. Evidence suggests that coaching is one of the most effective developmental tools in schools in terms of long-term impact. As coaching is based on the idea that all staff have the potential to develop each other, it serves to raise self-esteem and build the capacity for sustained improvement within a school.

Electronic resources

Go to www.sagepub.co.uk/allison for electronic resources for this chapter

Coaching helps people to …

Coaching is based on …

Skills–motivation matrix

Why coaching? 1

Why coaching? 2

Further reading

Joyce, B. and Showers, B. (2002) *Designing Training and Peer Coaching: Our Need for Learning.* Alexandria, VA: Association for Supervision and Curriculum Development.

Kelly, S. (2007) *The CPD Coordinator's Toolkit.* London: Paul Chapman Publishing.

3

Getting started

In this chapter we will look at:

- practising your coaching skills
- how to establish the ground rules for coaching
- conducting a coaching conversation
- how to give feedback on an observed lesson.

Practising your skills

We are assuming that as somebody working in a school, who is about to embark on some work as a coach, you will have received some training in the skills and principles behind coaching as outlined in the previous chapters. Perhaps your school has invested in the services of an external trainer for a group of colleagues or has introduced coaching to the whole staff on a training day. (See Chapter 8 for some ideas about how to train teachers in coaching techniques.)

So, you are ready to begin. You may well be feeling anxious and reticent about taking the first steps – after all, you are no expert and don't feel up to solving the classroom problems of your colleagues. You have enough of your own! Of course, you understand that coaching is not about having the answers or specific subject expertise, but even so … This is where your fellow coaches come in. They may be members of your small coaching group or indeed the whole staff. We suggest that you begin working in a coaching trio with two fellow coaches as described below.

Within the trio, one person will act as a coach and use one of the coaching models already described (STRIDE, FLOW or one of the others), to support the coachee with an issue that is real to them. This is very important. This work does not involve role play, rather it is dealing with real professional challenges. The observer will listen to the conversation and take notes. You may decide that the observer should act as *the coach's coach*, in order to suggest alternative questions. It is useful to note the body language of both parties, tone of voice, how naturally the conversation seems to flow, whether the coach brings out the solution or resorts to 'telling' the coachee what to do, and the types of questions that are being asked – are they open or closed? Which questions move the issue forward? The three people would subsequently swap roles,

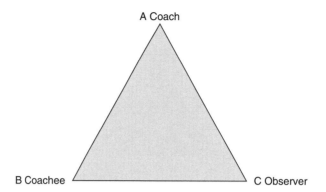

Figure 3.1   Coaching trios to develop coaching skills

until all three have had the opportunity to be coach, coachee and observer and have each had feedback about their performance as coach. You may have encountered the power of trios in your training. Certainly, in our experience, they are invaluable in the early stages of learning how to become an effective coach.

📁 Case study: Littlehampton Community School – Introduction to coaching

A mixed comprehensive school on the south coast of England, with approximately 1800 students on roll.

When coaching was first launched at Littlehampton, a group of 12 teachers were identified and provided with initial training in coaching, during which they experienced working in trios. The teachers within the group came from a variety of subject areas and had a wide range of experience. Some were in their first years of teaching and others were middle leaders. However, they were all good classroom practitioners and exhibited many of the skills and qualities of a good coach as described in previous chapters.

Before they went 'live' and worked with colleagues in school, it was clear that they needed to gain further experience in coaching and being coached outside of this training session. Even with all the necessary theory, coaches will only become effective once they have coached and been coached themselves. To this end, the coaches spent a summer term coaching each other. This gave them the opportunity to practise and refine their coaching skills.

During this training and development stage it is important to provide the coaches with the opportunity to meet up and discuss progress. This is a really important and necessary stage of the process. It is only once people have had a chance to do some 'real' coaching, that they come up with such issues as:

- How do we deal with long pauses?
- What happens when the conversation ranges over issues outside of school and starts to slip towards counselling?
- What happens if I don't know the answer?

The interesting point was that the coaches were now in a position to coach themselves to answer these questions. They also commented that they felt reassured having had the opportunity to make mistakes in a safe and supportive environment.

As the confidence of the coaches grows, staff could be offered the opportunity to work alongside one of the coaches. This then allows the coaches to put their skills to work on colleagues with real issues that need resolving.

How to establish the ground rules for coaching conversations

Once you have decided to begin to engage in coaching and you are about to enter a coaching partnership, you will need to give some thought to the basic ground rules with which coaching conversations will be conducted. Protocols are important, as they clarify the parameters within which you are working. Coaching is a very personal, and sometimes sensitive, process. So, if people are going to engage with it, they need to feel secure in, for example, the knowledge that their confidentiality will be respected. If this is not the case, they will not engage and you will go nowhere with it. (For suggestions about how to set up whole-school protocols, see Chapter 8.)

We recommend that you sit down with your coaching partner at your first meeting and agree a set of simple ways of working with which you both feel comfortable and which address some of the following questions:

- Will your discussions be confidential? (We assume that they will be!)

- Where and when do you intend to meet?

- What is to be the focus of the work? For example, are you looking to coach each other in specific aspects of your practice (co-coaching) or is one person primarily looking to use the other to bounce ideas off in order to clarify issues and commit to action? Perhaps your colleague is hoping to use you as a specialist coach, in order to achieve a performance management target. We assume that, whatever the emphasis, you will be keen to establish that this is a collaborative, non-judgemental and non-hierarchical process.

- What do you both want as desired outcomes of the coaching partnership?

- Is your work going to be time-limited? If so, how long do you intend to work together?

- How are you going to keep a record of the conversations? Are you going to use some sort of recording template (see Chapter 10)?

- If your work is going to involve classroom visits or lesson observations, how will you organise them (see below)?

- How will you evaluate the impact of the coaching on your practice?

- Your school may ask you for feedback on the value of the coaching process. How are you going to provide this? Are you being asked to fill in a questionnaire or some kind of summary sheet that gives an indication of the areas of your work? If so, will you do this independently or jointly? How does this sit with the principle of confidentiality? We deal with this issue in some detail in Chapter 10 and take the view that any account of coaching that is given to a third party needs to be carefully worded jointly by coach and coachee and should respect the agreed confidences between them.

Your school may have devised a protocol for coaching which deals with some of these questions. Although this may seem rather formal, it can be useful in that it serves to outline what the process is and how it would work. The other advantage of this approach is that it acts as a prompt, an ice-breaker, to generate discussion on what coaching is all about before you begin.

Conducting a coaching conversation

Of course, a coaching conversation is not a scripted event. It should be allowed to flow and will contain important silences as the coachee grapples with ideas and uncertainties. In the early stages, it will be important to build rapport and here the coach needs to demonstrate some of those key qualities that we identified in Chapter 2, notably respect for the coachee, a strong belief that the coachee has the solutions within himself or herself, genuine curiosity and unfailing optimism.

It is possible to manage some of the factors that impinge on the conversation, notably the environment in which the conversation takes place and your own responses to your colleague – how you listen, your physical posture and your tone of voice. In addition you have in mind a model for the conversation (STRIDE, FLOW, HILDA, and so on) that will help to give the dialogue some shape, as well as some useful questions that you hope to be able to ask at appropriate moments! Let's have a look at each of these factors in a little more detail.

The environment

Clearly you will need to find a room in which you can establish a comfortable yet professional atmosphere. Perhaps easy chairs will be available, water to drink and maybe a low table between you if you suspect your colleague may need a 'barrier', at least to begin with. It will be important to make and sustain good eye contact, so check that there is no excessive glare in the room. Ensure that you are not likely to be interrupted by people knocking on the door or by telephone calls and if you make notes, do so discreetly and with the coachee's permission.

Listening, physical posture and tone of voice

In Chapter 1 we discussed the importance of active, client-focused listening, as opposed to listening to the conversation inside your own head. At the outset this will be crucial in order to build rapport and to enable you to begin to tune in to the speech patterns and body language of your colleague. The messages that we give physically through how we sit in relation to other people are signals that we ignore at our peril when coaching. This is best illustrated through an example.

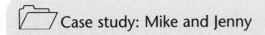

Case study: Mike and Jenny

Mike was to give coaching feedback on one of Jenny's lessons that he had observed. He had worked closely with Jenny for over a year or so and had established good rapport with her. Jenny was the Head of Humanities, and in her seventh year of teaching. The location for the conversation was ideal – easy chairs with a low coffee table between them, and the lesson had been really interesting. So he launched in enthusiastically with the first question, 'How do you think that went, Jenny?', leaning forward across the table as he spoke. Immediately, Jenny sat back and withdrew her legs under her chair, thus displaying a degree of discomfort. Over the next few moments Mike slowly sat back to reflect Jenny's seating position. As the conversation developed, Jenny moved forward in her seat as she identified the good practice that had been evident in the lesson and her confidence grew. By the end of the meeting she was thinking about how she might use what she was doing with other members of her department. Jenny and Mike were sitting with heads and torsos inclined towards each other across the table.

This is called *mirroring* and the important thing to note is that the coach, unlike Mike at the start of the conversation, must take his or her physical cues from the coachee. It really does put people at their ease, if done gently. It is a technique that needs practice and is something that you could work on with fellow coaches in a supportive trio.

Similarly you can tune or modify your tone of voice. For some people, as politicians will avow, this is a difficult area! You will need to adopt a natural, positive tone that encourages the coachee to relax, to say more and to reflect. Again, this is perhaps something that you could work on with coaching colleagues in a trio. Try an exercise in which the observer gives feedback examples of good (and then not-so-good) vocal tone and discuss the impact of each on the coachee.

The 'shape' of the conversation

Much of this book is about what the literature calls 'solution-focused coaching'. Essentially, the coach encourages the coachee to work *away from* a problem and *towards* a solution. As you will see in the examples below, the coach is constantly working to help the coachee to replace *negative self-talk*, which takes the form of 'can't do' statements, with *positive self-talk* ('can do'). This helps the coachee to avoid being stuck merely describing problems rather than looking for solutions. By encouraging this positive mindset, the coach is giving the coachee the confidence to move forward.

When conducting a conversation, we suggest that you try to avoid 'why?' questions, which can sound critical and may lead to defensiveness. Far better to ask, 'What led you to …', rather than '*Why* did you start the lesson like that?'. Similarly, 'What makes you think that …?' is a good substitute for '*Why* do you think that …?'

Be aware that the journey to a solution will not necessarily be a direct one. There may be cul de sacs and diversions on the way. Nevertheless, whichever model for coaching you have in your head, you are aiming to help the coachee to move through the following stages.

Setting goals

In this phase you are helping the coachee to formulate a desired outcome. Here, as elsewhere in the process, it will be important to help your colleague to see possible solutions rather than problems, so it is useful to avoid questions such as, 'What is the issue?' (problem focused) in favour of, 'What will it be like when you achieve your goal?' (positive focus). You are trying to help the coachee to tune into a *preferred future state*. Interestingly, the real goal may not be the first one that the coachee expresses. Be prepared to ask 'What else?', and to return to goal setting later in the conversation if necessary, as your colleague talks and reflects.

Checking the current reality

Try to keep the focus on the positive aspects of the present situation. You may be able to use the technique called *scaling* here to mitigate such totally negative self-talk as, 'I'm never successful with 8A' or, 'I can't do plenaries'. Try asking, 'On a scale of 1 to 10, how successful are you right now with 8A?'. Very few people will say 'zero' so the next question is, 'You say you are working at 3, so what features are effective to make it a 3?' and remember that positive tone of voice! In other words you are asking, what is already working, if only to a small degree? By asking such questions you are likely to discover, and enable the coachee to identify, some of his or her strengths and thus he or she will grow in confidence.

Considering options for action

Here you are helping the coachee to open up alternatives beyond the present, apparently restricted situation. You could, of course, ask 'What are your options in planning your next lesson for 8A?'. However, if you think it advantageous to help the coachee to stay in a positive future state, you might ask 'If 8A were working well, what would be happening?' or 'If there were no obstacles, what would you do?'. These are what Will Thomas calls *incisive questions* that may help your colleague to cut through to the nub of what success looks like. You could then move on to 'What might be the easiest (or most effective) thing to do?'. (See Chapter 2 of Will Thomas's book, *Coaching Solutions: Resource Book* (2005), for a helpful taxonomy of questions that could be used in coaching conversations.)

Committing to action

Having heard your colleague weighing up several possibilities, it is now time to ask, 'What do you reckon is the first step?' or a similar question designed to begin the process of focusing on action. Summing up could be useful at this point, during which you use the coachee's own words to reflect what he or she has decided to do. (Be prepared to summarise or reflect back what you have heard at any stage in the conversation. It is a useful check of whether you have understood and, for the coachee, whether he or she has communicated what they intended.) Once more you could ask your colleague to scale, this time as a measure of commitment. The answer to a question such as, 'On a scale of 1 to 10, how committed are you to doing this?', will speak volumes! If the answer is 'Probably 3', you will need to help your colleague to explore alternatives. You may even have to check reality by asking, 'What are the barriers to you doing this?'.

Revisiting the goal

Before the conversation ends it may be useful to reflect back to your colleague the stated goal from earlier in the conversation and then to ask, 'Is this a good place to start?'. You will be amazed how many times this question will lead to the response, 'Well, maybe I would be better doing ___ first'. But of course you must not imply that it is, or isn't, a good place to start. Here you need to keep your voice scrupulously neutral. In subsequent meetings you will need to help your colleague to evaluate the impact of his or her actions and perhaps to set further goals.

Finally, before you agree the date and time of the next meeting, remember to 'keep the door open', by saying something like, 'Let me know how you get on'. This will encourage informal, 'on the hoof' feedback and is an important signal of your genuine interest in your colleague's progress.

Giving feedback on an observed lesson

Clearly lesson observation is not a necessary part of coaching, although it often is part of the process. It is important that the purpose of the observation is clear. Is this an opportunity for the *coach* to be observed, in order for the coachee to see an aspect of pedagogy being demonstrated? If so, formal feedback may not be necessary or, if it is, it will involve coachee and coach de-constructing the lesson together in order to make explicit some aspect of practice.

Assuming that the purpose is the more usual one – that of coach observing coachee to subsequently ask questions, so that the coachee will focus on aspects of practice to be developed – we recommend the following positive, non-judgemental approach to the observation and feedback. It is very important to establish this non-judgemental approach to observing lessons from the outset. In practice we find that teachers find this very hard to do, and this is partly why we encourage coaches to observe each other and to give the sort of feedback described below, before they work with 'real' coachees.

Observing the lesson

- Negotiate the date, time and class to be observed and agree the focus of the observation.

- Greet your colleague and the children on entering the classroom unless you judge that this would disrupt the lesson.

- Give thought to where you will sit in the classroom in order to be least intrusive.

- Spend the first few minutes of the observation 'tuning in' to the class. Avoid making eye contact at this stage in order to allow your colleague and the children to behave as normally as possible. (It may be helpful to record any factual information at the top of your observation form during this phase.)

- You may wish to talk unobtrusively to children about their work, during an active part of the lesson. (Note the time during which you were not observing on the lesson record.)

- It may be useful to observe discreetly two or three members of the class to ascertain whether they are actively participating in the lesson and making progress.

- Write down exactly who does and says what and when in the lesson. The record of the lesson is a factual account of what takes place.

- An account of classroom dialogue can be useful as an aid to recall when giving feedback.

- It is helpful to record a timeline during the observation and to log the times at which significant or unusual events take place (for example, '2.15: child entered with note' or '10.05: practical activity began'). This helps the observee to map the passing of time. Bear in mind that managing time is a demanding skill for most teachers.

- With practice you will develop a personal shorthand that will enable you to record as much of what takes place as possible. Even then you will be able to record no more than about two thirds of what occurs.

- At the end of the lesson thank your colleague once all the children have left the room and confirm the time and place for the feedback. Do not be drawn into offering judgements about the lesson.

Giving feedback

- The feedback needs to take place as soon as possible after the observation (certainly within five working days), in private and in a relaxed atmosphere. It can be useful to provide the feedback in the room in which the observation took place in order to recall individual children by indicating where they were sitting. Do, however, give yourself thinking time beforehand. You may need to frame specific questions as a result of what you saw.

- Begin by asking your colleague how the lesson went. This often enables the teacher to express concerns about details of the lesson and to relax. Active listening is important at this stage.

- As in any coaching conversation, be aware of your colleague's body language during the feedback. It is effective to gently mirror his or her posture as the session progresses.

- Start *by saying something positive in the first sentence of the feedback*. Then recount the observation record in a matter-of-fact way, stopping as necessary to give and receive comments and to ask questions for clarification.

- Remember to maintain good eye contact with your colleague during your feedback.

- Be descriptive rather than judgemental and avoid 'you should have …' statements.

- It is important to focus on what happened in the lesson. In this method of giving feedback *the observer is acting as a mirror* to enable the coachee to see the lesson and to draw conclusions for herself or himself.

- It can be useful to model the way in which your colleague did or said something during the lesson. This technique should be used with caution and only in a secure, professional, coaching relationship and with the coachee's permission.

- As issues emerge, ask questions that will enable the coachee to open up possibilities for change. For example, 'What would it have looked like if …?' and 'What led you to …?'. Sometimes the teacher will make a statement that can be explored with the question 'Could you tell me a bit more about …?'. Alternatively, it may be helpful to reflect something that he or she said earlier in the conversation. In other words, use your coaching skills.

- At the end of the feedback the observee should be encouraged to reflect on the feedback and to draw out the strengths of the lesson and any issues that he or she wishes to tackle. 'So, what do you now feel about the lesson?' or 'What did you see in the feedback?' or 'What do you think having heard the feedback?' are all useful ways of encouraging this self-reflection.

- The coachee may decide, as a result of the coach's questioning, to specify targets to be worked on subsequently.

- A copy of the observation record may be given to the observee. It is also helpful for the coach to provide a written summary of the observation. This should state the strengths of the lesson and any actions that the coachee intends to take. It should be a summary of the points raised in the feedback and should contain nothing new. It may be useful to leave the coachee with one or two questions during the feedback to prompt reflection. These questions should be written in the summary.

- At the end of the feedback both parties should feel positive about the experience.

- If further observations are planned, the coach must allow sufficient time to elapse before returning. In the meantime, updates and advice can be exchanged informally in the staff room. It is important to allow the coachee time to consolidate the skills that have been targeted. Teachers, like other learners, may regress before they progress!

Questions for reflection and discussion

- Which coaching skills do I currently use in my work?
- Which coaching skills do I need to develop?
- How will I do this?
- What support is to be provided for coaches in the early stages of their work?

Summary

- It is important to find opportunities to practise your coaching skills before 'going live' with coachees.

- Coaches need to pay attention to the environment in which they hold coaching conversations as well as to their physical posture and tone of voice.

- They also need to establish some mutually acceptable ground rules for the coaching work.

- It is important to keep in mind the 'shape' of the conversation when coaching.

- When giving feedback on observed lessons as a coach, concentrate on giving a factual account of what happens in the lesson.

Electronic resources

Go to www.sagepub.co.uk/allison for electronic resources for this chapter

Record of coaching conversation (FLOW)

Record of coaching conversation (STRIDE)

Self-talk and performance success task

Further reading

Flaherty, J. (1999) *Coaching: Evoking Excellence in Others.* London: Butterworth-Heinemann.

Starr, J. (2003) *The Coaching Manual.* London: Prentice Hall Business.

Thomas, W. (2005) *Coaching Solutions: Resource Book.* Stafford: Network Educational Press.

Specialist coaching

In this chapter we will look at:

- what we mean by specialist coaching
- how school leaders can use specialist coaching to address specific developmental priorities within their school
- how coaching can play an integral role in performance management
- the wider issues of collaborative working within schools.

As part of a school's own self-evaluation, there will be specific areas of teaching and learning that will be highlighted as areas for development and these will be included in the school's development plan. It is at this stage that there is often a gap. Having identified areas for development, schools do not always make adequate provision to address the issues. At best, there may be a slot during a staff training day to explore the issue. It is unlikely, however, that this will be followed up in any widespread and sustained way and, as a result, the momentum usually gets lost. At worst, it may be left to chance for this area of weakness to become an area of strength – this will very rarely happen.

Specialist coaching allows schools to address these specific issues in a targeted and sustained way. When we refer to specialist coaching, we are talking about teachers who have a strength in a particular area, for example behaviour management, working alongside and coaching colleagues who want to develop this area of their practice. This approach can be used to develop specific areas of teaching and learning, such as how to give effective instructions or how to check what has been learned during a lesson. These will be seen as key areas that need to be developed within the school and will of course vary from one school to another. Staff who are known to be good practitioners in these areas can then be asked if they would be willing to work with colleagues as coaches. This approach requires schools to have effective monitoring systems in place enabling them to identify who amongst their teaching staff is good at what. In our experience, when staff are offered the opportunity to work with a coach on specific areas of teaching and learning – as opposed to a more generic offer of coaching – the response has been positive. Why? This is not clear, but one possible reason, emerging from discussions with staff, is that it takes away the need for teachers to identify an area that they need to develop – it is done for them.

This approach can be taken a stage further, and in one school we have worked with it has now become an integral part of the performance management process. This could be seen as a contentious approach by those who hold the view that coaching has no role to play in performance management. We would argue, strongly, that this does not need to be the case. Performance management should be about setting challenging and professional targets for teachers that will develop them professionally and improve standards in schools. However, this should be strongly underpinned by looking at how the professional development needs of staff will be met to enable them to reach these targets. This is where coaching comes in. It is one of many professional development activities that can be offered to staff, to help them address these targets. The recent review of performance management arrangements in England (Rewards and Incentives Group, 2007) has gone a long way to addressing this by making it obligatory for reviewers to devise a CPD action plan for individuals when setting their performance management targets. Furthermore, if the performance management process is to be a success, all parties concerned need to have a sense of ownership over it. If it is simply something that is 'done to you', then people are less likely to engage with it and strive to meet the targets that may be set. With this in mind, the performance management meeting between the reviewer and reviewee should be run like a coaching session where the reviewee is encouraged to find the solutions to help them meet their objectives themselves.

 Question for reflection and discussion

Performance management should be a key driver for delivering the school development plan and focusing on the professional development needs of the staff. To what extent is this the case in your school?

Coaching can play two important roles in the performance management process.

1   It encourages the reviewee to come up with their own developmental targets and ways of addressing them during the planning meeting. The reviewer becomes the coach and the reviewee becomes the coachee. As a result, the reviewee feels a greater sense of ownership in the process and is therefore more likely to engage with it.

2   It serves as a developmental activity to support staff in achieving their targets – for example, the provision of specialist coaching in an aspect of pedagogy and practice.

 Case study: Littlehampton Community School – performance management

At Littlehampton, when colleagues carry out their Performance Management Planning/Review Meeting, they complete a CPD action plan. As part of this, they are offered the opportunity to work alongside a coach on any aspect of teaching and learning that they wish to develop. Alternatively, they can opt to work with a specialist coach on one of the following aspects of teaching and learning:

- assessment for learning
- behaviour for learning

(Continued)

(Continued)

- developing literacy skills
- using Information Technology as an effective teaching and learning tool.

Interestingly, this tied in with one of the requests made by teaching staff on how they would like to see coaching progress at the school – a number of staff stated that all teachers should be offered the opportunity to work alongside a coach. In terms of opening up coaching, this has been extremely successful. At least 50% of those who returned their CPD action plans, following their performance review meetings, asked either to work alongside a coach in a specific area, or to observe a colleague teaching with a view to focusing on an area of their teaching that they wish to develop. The latter will tend to result in the development of a coaching relationship.

The success of this approach was further aided by time being put aside on a school closure day for colleagues to meet and have their review meetings and complete their CPD action plans. This, in our minds, is an essential part of the process. If we want the process of performance management, and the associated discussions regarding CPD, to become an effective coaching conversation, then schools need to give staff the time to carry out the process in a relaxed and stress-free atmosphere. Only then will meaningful discussions take place that may then lead to positive outcomes. This is not necessarily the case if the performance management process takes place after a busy day of teaching. Coaching takes time.

Those who are carrying out the performance management review meetings will need some guidance on how the meetings should run, in order to achieve more of a coaching focus. If this is not done, then they may well revert to form and end up telling the reviewee what they need to do better and how. Firstly, they will all need to have had some training in the principles and skills of coaching. Secondly, they will need to be fully briefed on how the meetings should run within a coaching model. This will almost certainly require some briefing sessions with the reviewers, before they embark on their meetings. This investment in time beforehand will pay dividends in terms of the quality of the performance management process.

The important role of the CPD co-ordinator in setting up coaching, has been discussed elsewhere in this book. This role becomes pivotal if a performance management process that is linked to CPD, such as the one described at Littlehampton, is to be successful. Here teaching staff hand their CPD action plans to the CPD co-ordinator, who is then charged with analysing the many coaching requests on these plans and with pairing colleagues up accordingly. Clearly, this can only be effective if the school has a very good working knowledge of the strengths of its teaching staff – and this will only be the case if the school has a strong self-evaluation structure in place.

At Littlehampton, the long-term plan was always to dovetail the processes of school self-evaluation, the school development plan, performance management and CPD. Incorporating the CPD action plan into the performance management process seemed to be the final part of the jigsaw.

It is clear to see how coaching, particularly specialist coaching, plays a key role throughout this process.

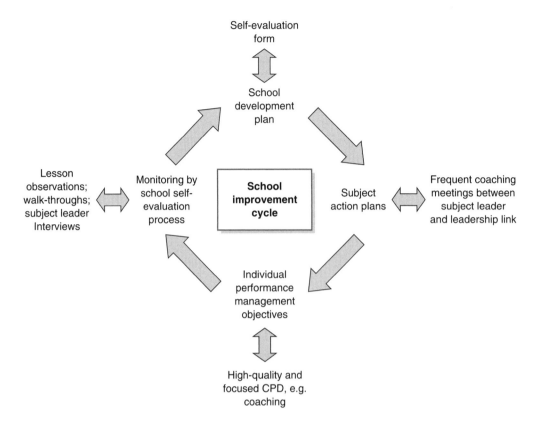

Figure 4.1   School improvement cycle

- The school development plan, based on developmental priorities from the self-evaluation form, feeds into subject action plans. Within these plans, subject teams identify how they will address specific whole-school developmental priorities. For many subjects, this may involve setting up a peer-coaching programme or focusing on a specific area of teaching and learning, for example, assessment for learning. The subject leaders then meet regularly with a leadership link (somebody from the school leadership team) to be coached on leading this process.

- These subject action plans form a framework for teachers to focus on their individual developmental needs during their performance management review meetings. As a part of this process, they complete their CPD action plan and can opt to work with a specialist coach in that area, for example assessment for learning, from a different subject.

- During the monitoring process, school leaders and subject leaders observe lessons. While making a judgement on the quality of teaching and learning is a key part of this process, more important is the coaching conversation between the observer and the teacher that should happen following the observation.

This can be further developed at Littlehampton, with a view to having a whole-school push on consistency of approach, in terms of classroom practice, in the following key areas:

- Teaching for Learning

- Assessment for Learning (AfL)

- Behaviour for Learning

- Literacy for Learning.

 Case study: Littlehampton Community School – The Learning Toolkit

In order to achieve this integrated process of school self-evaluation, school development, performance management and CPD at Littlehampton, a document has been produced called 'The Learning Toolkit'. This is a key document for the school in terms of outlining what is expected in terms of effective teaching and learning. It contains four sections – on Teaching for Learning, Assessment for Learning, Behaviour for Learning, and Literacy for Learning – and each section is then divided into key sub-sections:

- Principles – the importance of the approach
- Practice – what the principles should look like in the classroom
- Strategies – suggested strategies to help put the principles into practice.

Specialist coaching is being used to support teachers at the school to turn the principles within the document into practice. Three teachers have been appointed to a coaching role, called 'professional tutors'. Each of these professional tutors has been allocated to a cluster of subject areas, and is then charged with using their coaching skills to support the subject leader in embedding the aspects of the toolkit into the day-to-day teaching within that area. The school self-evaluation process is used to identify areas of need, where this specialist coaching can then be targeted. Furthermore, the coaches will facilitate the sharing of best practice between subject areas within their clusters. So, for example, if a teacher in history is very skilled at developing the literacy skills of low-ability students, he or she should be asked to coach a teacher in science who wishes to develop this aspect of teaching and learning.

There is also evidence of specialist coaching being used within teams. The science department at Littlehampton Community School has identified AfL as being a key priority for development this year. The subject leaders for science have bought in some excellent AfL resources, however they are mindful of the fact that it is not enough to just buy the resources – they have to become embedded into the teaching of all science teachers. To facilitate this, they have identified teachers within the team who demonstrate good AfL practice. These colleagues have then been paired up with other science teachers. The pairs will then co-plan an AfL-rich lesson using the new resources. They will observe each other delivering the lesson, then feed back to each other in a coaching style. The best practice will then be shared with the whole department, during departmental meeting time.

Another example of this sharing of expertise has been seen with the English department and other departments within the school. Following an after-school session on developing literacy strategies, members of the English

(Continued)

(Continued)

department paired up with colleagues from the geography department who wanted to develop literacy strategies within their subject. The colleagues within the English department then coached their colleagues by co-planning a literacy-based activity with them. They then observed the activity in action in the classroom, followed by a coaching conversation after the lesson on the effectiveness of the strategy.

 Question for reflection and discussion

Does your school have systems in place to facilitate the sharing of best practice amongst the staff?

It is clear that the landscape of school leadership is changing towards a more collaborative approach between schools. In order to prepare our future leaders for this, we need to facilitate this process within schools and encourage colleagues to move outside of the comfort zone of their own subject areas – especially in large secondary schools. Specialist coaching provides us with the opportunity to do this by encouraging colleagues from one subject area who wish to develop an aspect of their practice, to work with a good practitioner in this aspect of practice from a different subject area.

This should not be left to chance. In smaller primary schools, it tends to happen quite naturally due to a lack of subject-based compartmentalisation – and the most effective primary schools ensure that it happens regularly. Secondary schools need to re-evaluate how they structure themselves, in order to move towards a more effective, internal collaborative approach and this may involve asking questions about the effectiveness of subject-based compartmentalisation.

A common structure for secondary schools is the faculty structure. In this model, subjects with some commonality – for example, physical education, drama, dance and so on – are placed together, often with a head of faculty and then heads of department beneath that. This may work fine. However, if the subjects within that faculty are not working effectively, then who can colleagues learn from? This problem may be exacerbated if there are issues of poor leadership within that faculty. If the subjects within the faculty have all identified, for example, differentiation for the less able as a development priority, but then only ever meet together as a faculty group, how are they going to be able to learn from another subject area not in their faculty which demonstrates good practice in this area?

Would a more sensible alternative to the 'faculty' approach be to group subject areas together according to developmental needs, areas of strength and leadership capacity, irrespective of tenuous subject-based links? For example, why not group four or five unrelated subject areas together as 'school improvement teams'? Each of these small clusters of subjects could be strategically put together to include some subjects areas with strengths in certain areas of pedagogy, coupled with strong leadership, alongside other subject areas which need to develop certain areas of their practice, and which may lack the leadership capacity to drive this through. Amongst these school improvement teams could be set up some strong specialist coaching, based on pedagogy, avoiding an over-emphasis on subject-related issues. This model could be a very powerful driver for a more collaborative and effective form of middle leadership within secondary schools.

 Question for reflection and discussion

Does your school departmental structure facilitate the sharing of best practice and collaborative working between subject areas?

 Summary

School self-evaluation needs to be used to identify areas of whole-school developmental focus. There will then be a wealth of expertise within the staffroom that should be used in a coaching capacity to develop these areas of teaching and learning. The performance management process should also be used to enable staff to identify their CPD needs, with regards to these areas of focus, and then commit to action. Underlying all of this is the need for schools to look at their structures, systems and procedures to ensure that there are opportunities for staff to work collaboratively and share best practice.

5

Using coaching for new teachers

In this chapter we will look at:

- how co-coaching can be used to develop newly qualified teachers
- how coaching can be used to develop teachers in their second year of teaching.

Working with trainee and newly qualified teachers (NQTs) can be a highly rewarding part of the job. It is also often a privilege. Their energy and enthusiasm for teaching often translates into excellent classroom practice, even very early in their careers. They are usually highly reflective about what they do and eager to learn how to improve. They will question why things are done in 'that particular way' and not just accept the status quo. These attributes make for good coachees, but also good coaches.

Co-coaching has been described by CUREE (Centre for Use of Research and Evidence in Education) as 'a structured, sustained process between two or more professional learners to enable them to embed new knowledge and skills from specialist sources in day-to-day practice'. (Source: The National Framework for Mentoring and Coaching: CUREE)

With this in mind, it makes perfect sense to use co-coaching to support and develop the work of trainee and newly qualified teachers. Teachers early on in their careers have many questions as to how they might improve their practice and they also have many of the solutions. Mentors can answer many of these questions, and do a brilliant job. However, if we want to move away from dependency to independence, we need to encourage these young teachers to engage in coaching.

> **Question for reflection and discussion**
>
> Are NQTs given the opportunity to work collaboratively within your school?

The Career Entry Development Profile (CEDP), developed by the TDA (Training and Development Agency for schools, UK), is an online resource that encourages trainees and NQTs to focus on achievements and goals early on in their careers, and also to discuss their professional development needs. It does this by providing a series of questions for NQTs to reflect on at various stages in their training and induction periods. For example:

- What do you consider to be the most important professional development priorities for your induction period?

- Why are these issues the most important for you now?

- How have your priorities changed since the end of your training?

- How would you prioritise your needs across the induction period?

- What preparation, support or development opportunities do you feel would help you move forward with these priorities?

(Source: Career entry and development profile (CEDP) 2008/9: TDA)

This provides a perfect (and ready-made) framework to use when setting up co-coaching with NQTs. As well as discussing these questions with their mentor, they could also pair up and use them as prompts during the early stages of a co-coaching session.

Facilitating this process of NQTs working alongside their peers in co-coaching relationships is a very useful strategy which we decided to adopt at Littlehampton. The process was launched at an NQT meeting. Co-coaching was to be used for four main reasons:

- to encourage NQTs to discuss teaching and learning outside of their own subject

- to share best practice

- to raise self-esteem

- to encourage a 'can-do' approach.

The session started with a general discussion of what co-coaching was and why it could be useful. The NQTs were then asked to find partners (from a different subject to their own) and to ask each other the following questions:

- What is going well?

- What do I want to develop further?

They were told that they could not make any judgements and were to avoid giving ideas. They just had to focus on listening and asking open questions. There was a lot of very intense discussion going on. We then stopped to consider the rest of the process, which is outlined below.

NQT co-coaching: the process

1 Identification of issue

NQTs identify issues that they wish to address.

2 Initial meeting

NQTs select co-coachees to work with.

Pairs meet to discuss issues.

3 Observation

NQTs observe each other.

Focus is kept on the issue that has been identified. Elements of best practice are also noted.

4 Feedback meeting

Pairs meet to discuss the lesson observations, return to the original issues and share best practice.

5 Follow-up

Pairs may decide to do follow-up developmental activities related to their focus, for example visit another school that shows best practice in this area or observe other teachers.

Stages one and two had already been addressed during this initial meeting. For those pairs who found it difficult to find a focus for their discussion, prompt cards were provided. These simple cards have various teaching and learning themes noted on them and they were used by the pairs to prompt discussion on areas of strength and areas for development. Sample cards are provided in Figure 5.1. For many, these cards acted as a very useful prompt. In fact, they are now used widely throughout the school in a number of different contexts, for example NQT/mentoring meetings, performance management meetings and department meetings.

After the initial meeting, the pairs then had to arrange a time to observe each other. They were all very keen to do this. A simple lesson observation review sheet was used to focus the observation. This was completed by the teachers being observed beforehand, to highlight the areas that they wanted the observers to look for. During the observation, the observer then commented on these points. This kept the ownership of the issue with the teacher being observed, but also served to keep the observation focused. A template is provided in Figure 5.2 on page 40. This completed review sheet should not be copied and remains the property of the coachee.

Once they had observed each other, they met up again to have a mutual feedback session. It had been agreed that the feedback would focus on the issue that the NQT had identified as an area for development – the review sheet helped to focus the conversation on this. It was, however, fine to focus also on other aspects of good practice that were observed.

Most interesting was the follow-up that resulted from this process. One pair, that was focusing on assessment for learning strategies, arranged to observe another

Use of voice	Monitoring pupil progress
Inclusion – meeting all pupils' learning needs	Coping with workload
Engaging and maintaining pupils' interest	Clearly focused learning objectives
Questioning skills	Use of ICT
Managing activity transition	Knowledge of the National Curriculum
Differentiation	Subject knowledge
Working with learning support assistants	Managing class discussions
Effective body language	Record keeping
The three part lesson	Managing pupil behaviour
Effective lesson planning	Assessment for learning
Starters and plenaries	Using assessment data
Pace	Learning styles

Figure 5.1 Coaching prompt cards

Lesson observation review sheet

Name _____ Co-coach _____ Date _____

Key questions for the lesson – agreed by coach and coachee	Comments/Observations/Questions – from the coach and coachee

Figure 5.2   NQT co-coaching

 Photocopiable:
The Coaching Toolkit © Shaun Allison and Michael Harbour, 2009 (SAGE)

teacher, who was known to be very good at using learning objectives to drive the learning in his lesson. Another pair, interested in transition, went on a visit to one of the feeder primary schools.

The NQTs were asked to evaluate the experience by answering a short questionnaire. The questions used and some of their responses follow.

Has the process been useful? Why?
'It has been a very useful process because I was able to observe some of the same students as I had taught in my co-coaching class. This gave me the opportunity to observe those pupils in a different environment and to observe different techniques and strategies that I could incorporate into my lessons.'

'The process has been useful because observing another teacher and discussing it with them has given me ideas for my own teaching.'

'Really useful to watch a class I teach in another subject – and then to discuss strategies that work with them, with another NQT.'

What did you learn from the process?
'I have learnt that we are constantly developing and that we can all benefit from this experience. I have picked up new ideas and ways of both helping my teaching and also my behaviour management.'

'That other NQTs have similar issues to me, and that they can be resolved.'

'That I had a lot of the solutions to my issues already – I just had to think it through. Talking it through with someone else really helped.'

What good practice did you observe?
'I observed a colleague, teaching a year 8 class, with some of the pupils that I teach in there. He had a starter activity set up for them to complete straight away which really helped settle them down. He also kept them on task all lesson and had extension tasks for those who had finished the previous task.'

'The use of a seating plan. Students working independently, whilst the teacher facilitated the process.'

How will this impact on your own teaching?
'Using a starter activity as soon as they enter the room is something that I will use with my year 8 class; it helps settle them immediately and helps with the lesson. I will also make sure that all pupils are on task all of the time and that there is extra work for those pupils who finish their task.'

'I will give my students more time to work independently.'

'More student-focused teaching and less teacher-focused.'

Next steps: Will you develop this work further? If so, how?
'I could develop this work further by building up a range of starter and plenary activities that will engage the pupils straight away. I will also try to break my lessons up into micro-chunks so that pupils can focus on key areas at a time.'

'Work with my co-coach on implementing the use of the interactive white board into my own teaching.'

This whole process proved to be successful – it certainly managed to achieve all of the objectives that were set out at the start of the programme. The NQTs were all very positive about the experience. They learned a great deal from each other, and from themselves through self-reflection. While using coaching in this way for NQTs and trainee teachers is not a substitute for mentoring, it certainly adds another important element to the support and professional development that they are offered. From a school's point of view, it goes a long way towards building capacity for growth by developing staff who are better equipped to finding the solutions to their own issues.

Coaching for recently qualified teachers

In order not to lose the momentum with coaching amongst our NQTs, it has also become an integral part of our Early Professional Development (EPD) programme for Recently Qualified Teachers (RQTs), that is, teachers in their second year of teaching. It has always seemed bizarre, that in the UK at least, a large amount of time and energy is rightly invested in supporting teachers in their first year of teaching. However, for some reason, usually financial, much of this support is taken away during the second year, and these new teachers are then left to sink or swim. This is wrong. It is so important that we continue to support and develop these teachers, so that they can become as good as possible. The support offered needs to be personalised and different from the mentoring they received during their first year – but it still needs to be there. Coaching is the key to this.

At the end of their induction year, NQTs are asked to identify two or three areas of teaching and learning that they would like to develop. When they then begin their second year of teaching they are allocated a coach, who will support them in devising an action plan to address these issues. The coaches are allocated in consultation with each of the RQTs and may be somebody from the leadership group, their NQT mentor or a peer. They then meet up regularly, at least once every half-term, for a coaching conversation on how the work is going. The coaches are there purely to support the RQTs through this important developmental stage of their careers.

The issues that have been selected are many and varied. However, the most important aspect of the process is that they are chosen by the RQT themselves – so that they are real and in context. Some examples are:

- 'What effective strategies are there to support the learning of EAL (English as an Additional Language) students in my lessons?'

- 'Developing kinaesthetic maths activities to engage and motivate low-ability students.'

- 'How the Levels Mountains approach can be used in ICT to raise student awareness of assessment criteria.'

- 'Developing an effective bridging programme in science.'

> ⌇⌇ **Question for reflection and discussion**
>
> Following their NQT year, is there a structured programme of support and guidance available to second-year teachers in your school?

This is an important and pivotal piece of developmental work for these teachers, for which there should be some kind of formal professional recognition. Fortunately, the General Teaching Council (GTC) for England, has set up the Teacher Learning Academy (TLA), that gives teachers the opportunity to obtain this recognition. By submitting a short presentation of their learning journey, during which they have been supported by their coaches, the teachers receive certificated professional recognition for the developmental work they have carried out as a part of the school's EPD programme.

Another advantage of this approach is that it has proven to be a good introduction to the performance management process for these relatively new teachers. The areas that they choose to look at with their coach also tend to become part of their performance management targets, thereby providing them with another layer of support to help them meet their performance review objectives.

There are clear long-term advantages for a school that wants to establish a 'culture of coaching' with new teachers in this way. The more opportunities these new teachers are given to engage with co-coaching, the more they will be refining and developing their own coaching skills. This is a solid investment for any school, as these staff will then be able to continue to use these coaching skills with other members of staff as they become more experienced – a 'home-grown' approach to developing coaching within a school.

□ Summary

NQTs have the ability to co-coach each other, and should be encouraged to do so. As they are experiencing many of the same issues, they can also provide each other with the solutions. They can prove to be a valuable and effective resource for each other.

Coaching is also a very powerful tool for supporting teachers in their second year of teaching. It can provide them with the support and encouragement to set their own developmental targets and then address them with a clear and effective action plan.

Electronic resources

Go to www.sagepub.co.uk/allison for electronic resources for this chapter

Coaching prompt cards

NQT co-coaching – lesson observation review sheet

Useful websites

www.curee-paccts.com/

www.tda.gov.uk/teachers/induction/cedp.aspx

Group coaching

> **In this chapter we will look at:**
> - **what we mean by group coaching**
> - **the important links between adult learning and group coaching**
> - **how coaching can be used to develop groups of staff.**

Much of the coaching that has been discussed up until this point involves two (or three) people engaging in a coaching conversation. Group coaching takes this a stage further. It is where a group of staff identify a common issue or CPD need, which is then addressed in a group setting, usually facilitated by one or more colleagues – the coach or coaches. There is an important point to be made here. Anybody who is going to be facilitating such a group session needs to have a good understanding of how adults learn best. We must be very careful not to make the assumption that a good teacher who knows how to facilitate the learning of children will naturally be able to work in the same way and be effective with adults.

The field of adult learning was pioneered by Malcolm Knowles and colleagues (2005). He identified the following characteristics of adult learners:

- They are autonomous and self-directed so a group coach needs to facilitate their learning and to engage them actively in the learning process. The learning should be done 'with them' and not 'to them'.

- They have accumulated a foundation of life experiences and knowledge that will include professional knowledge. The coach needs to be able to draw this out and link it to the learning.

- They are goal-oriented. The coach, therefore, must show colleagues how the session will help them to achieve their goals.

- They are relevancy-oriented so the learning must be relevant to their role and of value to them.

- They are practical. What will they be able to take away from the session that will help them to do their job better?

These characteristics need to be considered by anyone who is planning a group coaching session in schools.

 Questions for reflection and discussion

- How could a school provide good quality time for group coaching sessions?
- How can the groups be brought together?

As we move towards a more personalised learning experience for pupils, it is important that we adopt a similar philosophy for the CPD needs of our staff. Schools have a very large and varied staff in terms of skills, experience and motivation – with this comes a wide range of development needs. It is therefore important that staff are given a range of CPD activities, including group coaching, to address these needs.

One approach to achieving this is to move away from the 'one size fits all' approach to traditional school closure days, where all teachers sit together in a hall and are presented with the same training. This time could be more effectively disaggregated into after-school twilight sessions.

 Case study: Littlehampton Community School – group coaching

This model has been adopted at Littlehampton to good effect. Staff choose six after-school twilight sessions (from a menu of about 60) to attend, instead of two whole-school closure days. Staff have seen this as a hugely positive and useful initiative.

One piece of feedback from the first year of the sessions was that it would be good to have strands of twilights for people at different stages of their careers. We addressed this, the next year, by having four. This was then extended to five strands for the following year – an assessment for learning strand has been added to reflect the importance of this aspect of teaching and learning in the School Development Plan.

The details of these sessions follow:

- **General**   Twilights in this strand address general pedagogical issues such as starters and plenaries, behaviour for learning, differentiation, literacy.
- **Assessment for learning**   A range of sessions AfL-based: using learning objectives, questioning skills, peer and self-assessment.
- **Developing excellence**   This strand of twilights is aimed at colleagues who may be interested in Advanced Skills Teacher (AST) or Excellent Teacher (ET) status and deals with such issues as brain-based learning and what makes outstanding learning.
- **Middle leaders**   Addressing issues that are specific to middle leaders such as managing and leading an intervention strategy, working with staff and improving learning in the subject.
- **Aspiring school leaders**   For middle leaders who are looking at whole-school leadership roles – includes topics such as The Production and Implementation of a School Development Plan and From Management to Leadership.

(Continued)

> *(Continued)*
>
> Departments are also offered the opportunity to run one of their own twilights, specific to their own needs and linked to the Department Development Plan. The teachers have responded very well to these sessions. Many staff commented favourably on being able to choose the focus for their CPD. The success of the sessions has been largely due to the fact that staff have a great deal of respect for their peers and have enjoyed hearing about how they have approached a particular issue. Having your own colleagues leading the sessions puts the topic into context and allows staff to follow up any issues with the person who led the session. This is usually not possible when you attend an external training course.
>
> At its inception, this model was never really intended to be a coaching-based initiative. It was simply a way of facilitating the sharing of best practice amongst staff. However, over the years, the sessions have certainly evolved into group coaching sessions. Although the people leading the sessions will have exhibited best practice in those particular fields, they do not claim to be experts. They are there to share their own practice and to facilitate discussion, sharing and learning among their peers. This is often done by posing challenging questions and encouraging colleagues to share their practice and find the solutions to their own problems – all attributes of effective coaching.

To ensure approaches, such as the one described at Littlehampton, work well in any setting, it is worth briefing the session facilitator on the following points:

- Enable all members of the group to have their say – draw out their experiences.

- Clarify what you hope to get out of the session – and, also, what they hope to get out of the session.

- Use challenging questioning.

- Encourage colleagues to listen to each other and reflect.

- Provide a sensitive and thorough explanation of the goals for the session.

- Make it clear that you are not the font of all knowledge, but are happy to share your experiences with them in order to develop their work.

- Encourage colleagues to commit to action!

So, when planning such a session, consider the following:

- Clear objectives for the session – what do you hope staff will get out of the session?

- Personal goals and 'live' issues – what do your colleagues hope to gain from the session? What concerns do they have about the issue that they would like to be explored during the session? Remember, it is fine if you don't have the answers, but what you can do is facilitate discussion within the group to help find a solution.

- Your perspective and experiences on the issues being discussed – you have been asked to lead the session because you have demonstrated best practice in this area. Share this with your colleagues – What works? What doesn't? What have you learned about the issue?

- Sharing the experiences of the whole group related to the issue – you will have a wealth of experience within your group – make sure you tease out and share all the good practice that already exists within it.

- Some kind of activity that involves colleagues working in small groups on a topic related to the issue.

- Time for group discussion – this is one of the most valuable elements of the sessions – the opportunity to discuss the issue with colleagues that you may not normally work with.

- A few concrete examples of strategies to go away and try in order to address the issue.

- Encouraging the group to commit to action! What are they going to do differently to address the issue?

As well as the obvious advantages of transferring new skills, there have also been a number of 'added bonuses' from these sessions:

- The self-esteem of staff has been raised as they are now facilitating the professional development of others. This makes them feel valued.

- We are beginning to see a shift in culture at the school – colleagues now feel more comfortable working outside their subject areas (a familiar problem in secondary schools).

- Pedagogy is no longer a dirty word.

- Staff feel a sense of ownership over their own CPD.

- Excellent value for money – the only costs involved in running such a programme are for tea, coffee and biscuits! However, we would argue that the impact is much greater than, for example, sending somebody on a course that costs £500 at a venue a hundred miles away.

It is worth exploring the other ways in which teams can use coaching to galvanise and develop themselves. In this sense, a 'team' can be a group of individuals with a common purpose but brought together for a variety of reasons such as:

- they all work within the same area, for example subject or pastoral teams

- they all have a similar role, for example middle leaders

- they all work in the same school.

Developing subject-based teams

Consider the following scenario:

 Case study: Initiating group coaching

A relatively new head of department inherited a fairly disparate group of people in the department. There was no collective vision for what good teaching and learning were like and very little sharing of best practice. This was a great shame, as many of the teachers in the department had a great deal to offer. Coupled with this, and for a variety of not unrelated reasons, morale was low. As a result, people had retreated back into their own classrooms and pretty much 'did their own thing'. Department meetings had become a combination of administrative announcements and tasks, and the downwardly spiralling discussion of the negative. Teaching and learning were off the agenda!

However, the head of department was also very conscious of the fact that the team needed a sense of ownership over the issues and the solutions. They also needed to be talking about pedagogy and sharing best practice. Most importantly, he wanted people to start to feel positive about themselves. So he established a peer observation programme.

The process began in a department meeting, where he opened up a discussion about what the team thought good teaching and learning looked like. The discussion began to flow and some key points began to emerge. Following the meeting, these were used to create a checklist of what the department thought a good lesson should look like. This was important in terms of the team having ownership over the issue. The head of department did not want to impose his views on the team – it needed to be a collaborative process. Not surprisingly, the list that they came up with was very similar to what the head of department would have suggested.

Armed with the collective criteria for good teaching and learning, the teachers were then paired up. This was done strategically, with good practitioners being put with colleagues for whom it was known that there were areas needing development. At the next meeting, the team was told of their pairings and that they had to observe each other teach. During the observations, they completed a tick-list for the criteria that they had all agreed on and these were returned to the head of department following the observations.

Most importantly, once the observations had been completed, each pair had to meet and have a conversation about the lessons. The staff were expected to ask each other two key questions:

- What went well?
- How would you make it even better?

Many other questions and a great deal of very useful discussion were also generated by these conversations. In one case, a NQT (who was excellent in the classroom) and a teacher with over 20 years' experience at the school, struck up a highly effective coaching relationship. They were often seen going in and out of each other's lessons in a very informal way, and then sharing their thoughts about what they had observed. This, in our minds, is when coaching is becoming embedded.

(Continued)

(Continued)

As a follow-up to this process, the head of department also analysed the tick-lists that were completed during the observations. The team then looked to see if the things that they thought made for effective teaching and learning were actually observed during the lessons. Of course, some were and some were not. This was fine, as the aspects that were not observed could then become an area of development for the whole department with a view to turning weaknesses into strengths. Again, the useful aspect of this approach was that the members of the team were, in effect, judging themselves. They had chosen the criteria, made a judgement about how effectively as a group they were meeting these criteria, and then devised some action points to address the deficiencies.

Developing middle leaders

Middle leaders play a pivotal role in the success, or failure, of a school. A good middle leader would be able to answer the following questions confidently:

- What is the quality of teaching and learning like in my team?

- What are our strengths?

- What do we need to improve?

- What have we improved over the last 12 to 18 months?

A middle leader who is struggling, for whatever reason, will find these questions difficult. This is where coaching can play an important role and, again, in a variety of different ways:

- If possible, enrol middle leaders on the National College for School Leadership programmes. Leading from the Middle and the newer programme, Leadership Pathways, both require middle leaders to carry out a diagnostic that looks at their leadership skills and qualities. They then work alongside a school-based coach to help them develop their leadership skills.

- Devise an in-house Middle Leader Development Programme where an experienced facilitator leads development sessions, examining the changing role of the middle leader. These sessions need not be presentations on how to do it, but rather sessions that require the leaders to work in groups to question each other in a supportive, yet challenging way.

- Change the way you run your subject leader meetings. Move away from dull, ineffective, information-driven meetings, with very little developmental discussion, towards meetings with a coaching focus. Have a key question for each meeting (for example, how can we develop effective plenaries?) and ask the middle leaders to question each other in pairs or trios on this issue, using the following prompts:

- What do you currently do that works?

- What would this look like if it was even better?

- What could you do to make it better?

- Develop a line-management structure that is based on a coaching relationship and ensure that meetings happen regularly. Each subject leader could have a leadership group link person whom they meet with once a fortnight. These meetings could have a developmental focus for the department and run like coaching conversations. This is important, as it builds capacity within the subject leaders and avoids a dependency culture where the subject leader simply seeks solutions from the leadership group link.

Developing the whole staff as a team

If, as a school leader, the aim is to develop a 'team ethos' amongst the staff, then it is sensible to use as many opportunities as possible to get staff working with colleagues that perhaps they would not usually work with.

- Staff meetings – in many institutions these need to be radically overhauled to have far more of a developmental focus. Why not sit staff in cross-curricular groups and discuss a specific issue important to the school, for example developing children's writing of explanations? Colleagues could then be encouraged to question each other in different subject areas with a view to sharing best practice. This could then be shared with the whole staff in a feedback session and disseminated within the subject teams.

- Inset days should offer opportunities to use coaching to share and disseminate best practice. A good way to do this is to use the 'Pedagogy and Practice' pack (2004), distributed to schools by the DfES (www.standards.dfes.gov.uk/secondary/keystage3/all/respub/sec_pptl0). Ask staff to choose one of the units that is of interest to them – there are 20, so there is plenty of choice. During the Inset day, in groups of people who opted for the same unit, ask each group to use the booklet and their own expertise to come up with a list of top tips for the topic in their unit. Once collated and distributed to all staff they make a very useful resource for staff to dip in to.

Case study: Bognor Regis Community College

A large 11–18 school with approximately 1600 students, Bognor Regis Community College wanted to develop the use of lesson starters during an Inset day. Six teachers were each asked to prepare an exemplar lesson that included a starter. The rest of the staff were then divided up into classes of approximately 15 people who rotated around these 'lessons', experiencing a range of different starters. Each lesson also included time to question the 'teacher' on the strategy, and staff then coached each other on how they could develop that particular starter activity in their lessons.

Summary

Group coaching can be an effective way to engage teachers in professional learning. It is also an effective team development tool. When implementing group coaching, ensure that those people facilitating the session have an appreciation and understanding of the principles of adult learning.

Further reading

Knowles, M., Holton, E. and Swanson, R. (2005) *The Adult Learner*. Boston, MA: Butterworth-Heinemann.

7

Coaching in challenging circumstances

> **This chapter is of particular interest to school leaders. In it we will:**
>
> - look at how two schools used coaching to help them to move out of special measures
> - consider how the coaching model may be used in different ways in challenging circumstances – for whole-staff training and for the development of the practice of individuals and departments.

The integrity of the coaching process can certainly come under pressure, and yet it can be a key to improvement in schools that are working in challenging circumstances, including those that have been categorised as requiring a Notice to Improve or Special Measures. Schools in such circumstances exhibit common features:

- Improvement in performance becomes urgent and school leaders begin looking for strategies that will have an immediate impact.

- Initially the school may enter a phase of denial and teachers will certainly experience a severe dip in morale. The self-esteem of even the most accomplished and confident teachers may take a tumble.

- Fairly quickly, if the school is to respond positively to its situation, key weaknesses in teaching and learning will be recognised and CPD arrangements will be put in place to support teachers in making rapid progress in, for example, delivering effective three-part lessons or introducing useful assessment strategies.

- As the process continues, teachers will begin to feel that they are being inspected and judged at every turn. They will therefore often welcome opportunities for professional dialogue without the risk of being graded 1 to 4.

This is where coaching can be crucial in helping colleagues to internalise rapidly the necessary skills that will lead, over a relatively short period of time, to significant improvements in teaching and learning. Given the right sort of leadership, teachers do become liberated by their situation and become willing to take *more* risks in the classroom than they might have done in normal circumstances.

The distinctions between mentoring and coaching may well become blurred as good practitioners seek to support colleagues who may feel, and indeed be, de-skilled.

Systems for running a coaching programme may be invented 'on the hoof' during or indeed after the event. The school should be pragmatic and use its good teachers to make a difference to the practice of others. Improvement in practice across a school with significant challenges can be dramatic if a climate of trust is created and when coaching and mentoring become central platforms, as the following case studies demonstrate.

Case study: The Mayfield School experience

A mixed comprehensive 11–16 school in Portsmouth.

Prior to being put into special measures, the school had unsuccessfully launched a peer coaching initiative. A group of good practitioners had been trained and a flyer had been produced inviting colleagues to participate but there had been little interest. With hindsight the school's CPD co-ordinator, Bill Whiting, and lead coach, Vicky Whitlock, felt that, at that time, teachers saw the need for coaching as a mark of failure and therefore did not sign up to it. However, the climate quickly changed with the advent of special measures. As Vicky observed, 'there was no fear – things couldn't get much worse than special measures – there was nothing to lose'. In these circumstances, 'people seek help more'.

Mayfield, in common with all schools, had a number of very good practitioners. By the end of the summer term, two years after special measures, an audit of the skills of these teachers had been conducted following observations of their lessons. The audit involved self-assessment against an inventory of classroom management and teaching skills. Each teacher was asked to decide what he or she was good at and what he or she could demonstrate to others. This inventory became a directory which colleagues are able to access when they need help with a particular aspect of their practice and 'the knowledge' was held by Bill Whiting, a long-serving and trusted colleague with whom staff felt comfortable and able to discuss their professional needs.

During the following academic year potential coaches met to share their practice and to explore the issues around peer coaching and mentoring colleagues. Early in the year, all teachers were invited to use the coaching 'service' and a protocol was established which clarified the ground rules by which coaches and coachees would operate. Four or five colleagues took up the opportunity and had positive experiences of the coaching process.

Each inexperienced teacher on the staff was offered a coach as a matter of course. The coach was, in principle, not a member of their department. This was done to avoid any feeling on the part of the inexperienced teachers that they were being assessed or inspected by the coaches in a climate where scrutiny and accountability were inevitably the norm.

Over two or three years the school had recruited untrained teachers, ten of whom qualified through the Graduate Teacher Training Programme. All of these

(Continued)

(Continued)

teachers were allocated a coach during their training and observed coaches teaching as part of their induction. Two of the coaches were trained in pupil behaviour modification and contributed to the graduates' programme and to whole-staff training to ensure that behaviour management was, as far as possible, based on consistent principles and to help teachers develop an appropriate repertoire of pupil management strategies.

At this stage, the impact of the coaching process was particularly marked for the graduate trainees and was evaluated both by lesson observation and by feedback from the graduate teachers themselves. Moreover, all the teachers who had offered their time to support others actually improved their own practice. This is not really a surprise. After all, they had to reflect on what they were doing in order to explain and demonstrate to others.

In the report which led to special measures being withdrawn from the school, three years after it was instigated, HMI observed: 'Many lessons taken by the new trainees were taught well and adhered to the good practice guidance issued by the school. The school has begun to tackle the long-term weaknesses in teaching with increased vigour'.

What happened next?

When HMI returned and confirmed that the school was continuing to make progress beyond special measures, they commented that the graduate training programme was 'successfully bringing a new group of teachers into the school'. They also stated, 'In addition, the lessons learned through this programme are being used effectively as the cornerstones of the school's continuing professional development (CPD) programme. Successful and experienced teachers have made a good impact as coaches and mentors in another innovative element of the CPD programme'. The success of the graduate trainees did not, of course, go unnoticed by the rest of the staff.

Beyond special measures and the use of coaching trios

The school had already arranged for 20 members of the coaching group to receive a day's training shortly after the final HMI visit. This experience was invaluable in making coaching skills explicit and in giving the team confidence that they were heading in the right direction.

Following this training it was decided to disseminate the good practice that was being developed in the school by organising the whole staff into coaching trios. CPD sessions were delivered on aspects of the teaching repertoire – assessment for learning, questioning, modelling and explaining – using coaching trios. Colleagues were asked to develop their practice by working together in a variety of ways including sharing ideas, joint planning, observing each other using a specific skill in the classroom, and helping each other to develop their repertoire by acting as critical friends (see Figure 7.1). These trios were:

- carefully balanced in terms of background and experience

- from three different departments

- given time to meet regularly to coach each other.

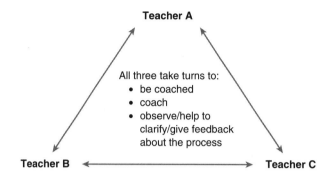

Figure 7.1   Coaching trios to develop the teaching repertoire

Bill Whiting used the audit of teaching and learning and his knowledge of the staff to ensure that the trios had the right sort of chemistry. He watched the process closely, took feedback from colleagues and adjusted the groupings when they did not appear to be functioning well. After working with two colleagues on assessment for learning, one teacher commented:

> It felt like someone had invented the thing I had been trying to create for some time. It was that powerful. We developed an assessment tool to use across all years and all abilities.

How coaching trios are put together will be a strategic decision for individual schools. You may wish to consider the following:

1   A, B and C are all equal – for example, they are good practitioners who are all looking to develop their coaching skills.

2   A, B and C are all from different subject areas within a school. One of these areas may be a strength of the school, whilst the other two may require some improvement.

3   A is a teacher with a particular talent in a specific area, for example using group work. B and C are teachers who wish (need) to develop this area.

At Mayfield it quickly became apparent that the colleagues in the most successful trios:

• gave each other confidence

• shared their ideas freely

• enabled each other to reflect on their teaching and to commit to trying out new strategies

• developed their coaching skills.

After the work on assessment for learning, a follow-up training day was arranged during which a range of practice was shared in a 'show and tell' session. This was highly significant. For example, the headteacher had been involved in one trio that had helped an outstanding graduate trainee to develop an excellent peer assessment strategy for her year 7 English class. She observed at the time:

You can learn so much from your peers. It's great to listen to other people's ideas and it's a great confidence booster when other people like yours. I was initially nervous about the idea of the coaching trio – particularly as I had the headteacher in my group.

Despite any initial nervousness, the experience was a success and the head's involvement indicated the importance that the school attached to coaching. Moreover, some of the ideas on show had been developed by colleagues whose practice was not seen as outstanding. So the message was clear – coaching works for all sorts of teachers at all levels of experience and is endorsed by the senior team.

After about a year, as colleagues moved on, the trios were seen to be losing their impact so Bill began to organise CPD coaching into groups of six in order to revitalise the sharing of good practice.

Three years on

Lessons were now being recorded on video for analysis in coaching conversations and the school had the technology to enable coaches to talk to teachers via an earpiece whilst lessons were being observed.

The school had developed a tightly knit coaching team that was managed by Vicky Whitlock, now an advanced skills teacher (AST), and had instituted a teaching and learning group which was useful in identifying pedagogical issues that could be addressed through one-to-one coaching or through the school's CPD arrangements. Performance management also routinely helped colleagues to identify needs for which they could volunteer for coaching.

On reflection, Bill likened coaching to a virus that adapts to the climate of the school. At Mayfield it had clearly gone through several 'mutations'. As the climate had improved, beyond special measures, people wanted to improve their practice and began to 'walk through the door' into the school's coaching programme.

Vicky's own practice had developed significantly. She noted that coaching had helped her to stop trying to soak up other people's problems like a sponge. She was now a mirror that reflected back. Coaching was about 'stepping into their coachee's world and seeing things from their perspective' and, by asking questions, enabling them to see their own problems and to find their own solutions. People solved problems for themselves in the long term, she said, so being coached was not a quick fix but a life-changing experience.

She was clear about the importance of helping her coachees to set their own targets and had developed an interesting strategy. At the end of a coaching conversation she would produce a small box into which the coachee would place the target for the week. The box, which could be held by either Vicky or her colleague would then be produced at the start of the next meeting and the coachee would remove the slip of paper and discuss whether the target had been achieved – a simple technique that is likely to increase the commitment of teachers to carry out their stated intentions.

Case study: Bognor Regis Community College and special measures

A large 11–18 school with approximately 1600 students.

After Bognor Regis Community College was placed in special measures, the school began by providing initial training for a group of 22 teachers who were seen as having the potential to become coaches. Soon afterwards Julia Vincent, deputy head and the CPD co-ordinator, announced a clear intention to train the whole staff, non-teachers and teachers alike. This goal was achieved within a year by withdrawing groups of about six colleagues at a time from their usual duties to receive training.

During special measures, Julia kept a database of the quality of teaching, and the school quickly developed a policy that teachers who were observed as unsatisfactory or at best satisfactory would be offered one of the school's four ASTs, or a peer coach from a different department, to support them in moving their practice to a satisfactory or good standard. In addition they would be mentored by a manager, usually their head of department or second in department. The headteacher made it clear that colleagues could reject the offer of coaching but not the departmental mentoring. In many cases teachers did take up the offer of coaching and a significant proportion improved their teaching so that, when observed, their lessons were judged to be satisfactory and sometimes good. As at Mayfield, the practice of the coaches rapidly improved so that they were regularly observed teaching lessons that were judged to be good or better.

Throughout this work, the coaches and ASTs operated a protocol of confidentiality, and they certainly did not make judgements about the coachees – this task was left to the appropriate managers. However, they did face the need, on occasions, to suggest a way forward or to demonstrate a skill, in effect to assume the role of mentor (see Chapter 2). As Julie Woodward, one of the coaching team at the time, reflected later, 'In a school, and particularly one in challenging circumstances, coaching and mentoring *is* blurred. Coaching shouldn't be judgemental but someone needs to be. Judgements have to be made'.

The coaches kept a log of their activities which was shared with their coachees and with Julia. By comparing the coaches' records of their work with the lesson feedback forms, including Ofsted judgements, that she was receiving from mentors and line managers, Julia was able to gain some measure of the impact of the coaching. Colleagues realised that this was important, given the special measures designation, and accepted the coaching logs as a necessary part of the school's evidence of improvement.

The school maintained clarity about who was being supportive and non-judgemental (that is, the coaches) and who was monitoring the progress of teaching and learning and making the necessary judgements. At all times these roles were kept separate.

At the end of special measures, when asked what the factors were that had enabled the school to improve its teaching and learning so quickly, one colleague summed up as follows:

> Being confident and wanting to deliver a lesson that was more than satisfactory. Through CPD, coaching, mentoring, modelling of good practice and self-evaluation, most colleagues recognised the features of a good lesson and were starting to feel confident that they could deliver to this standard.

After special measures: refocusing the coaching team

After successfully coming out of special measures, Julie Woodward and Sue Bond, both active coaches while the school was in special measures, were given joint responsibility, as lead coaches, to move the initiative forward. Julie was to lead on literacy and would be based in the upper school and Sue would lead developments on the lower school site.

Julia Vincent, Sue and Julie met with a group of 12 good practitioners, who had demonstrated their impact as coaches during special measures, to outline the strategy for re-launching coaching on the two sites. Initially, some coaches were to be deployed within clusters of departments in discrete zones in the lower school and others were to work alongside the ASTs and were allocated to specific departments in the upper school.

Support was provided by Lesley Smith from the local authority's School Improvement Service, who is a skilled trainer and coach. Her input was critical to the success of the coaches' work. She initially provided training by setting up coaching trios comprising members of the school's coaching team, each supported by herself. She encouraged the coaches to observe each other teaching, with a focus that was agreed in advance, and she then facilitated the feedback. She continued throughout the development of this team to coach the coaches and her interventions have been seen as highly significant in sustaining the confidence of the coaches and in helping them to refine and develop their skills.

Later, Trevor Pask, one of the team members, commented on how much he had learned from Lesley and from his colleagues in the trio and that a range of coaching conversations had ensued. Julie and Trevor agreed that this phase had helped to hone the coaches' skills, specifically around listening, questioning, avoiding 'telling' and tuning into the feelings of their peers, and by embedding a model for a coaching conversation. Significantly, Trevor felt that it had been important that the coaching team did not engage with the whole staff until they were comfortable with each other and with the coaching process.

The initial focus of their work had been with teachers of years 7 and 8 in the lower school, where teachers needed support to establish clear boundaries and to give a consistent message to students. This work had a positive impact but suspicion was growing that coaching may only be for weak practitioners. To address this, Julie and Sue pulled off a master stroke. They organised a staff training session, at which the coaching team stated who had coached them and in which aspects of their practice, before launching into role plays that demonstrated what coaching conversations looked like. Flyers were then sent out to all teachers stressing the confidentiality of the process and inviting them to participate in coaching. Photos of the coaches were displayed in both staffrooms as this is a split-site school.

Colleagues now felt more confident to put themselves forward and the message was clear – if you were a good practitioner, you would want to be coached. Throughout this phase, the coaches maintained the practice of keeping a simple log of the meetings but the content was deliberately not recorded. Details of the coaching process were not shared, except at the coachees' request.

Another impetus to the development of coaching was the work that the school was undertaking in developing literacy strategies (see the science department case study below). As Julie Woodward put it, 'for the literacy to work, it had to sit on a bed of coaching'.

The lead coaches developed several ideas that raised the profile of coaching in the school. For example, they provided teaching and learning boxes that contained useful materials to enable teachers to widen their repertoire, and they instituted Tell Forms that teachers were asked to complete when they had successfully tried out a new idea. Each week the department that had been the most innovative received a prize at the Friday staff briefing! These strategies helped to create a climate in which colleagues were willing to try out new ideas and to be coached in applying them.

The lead coaches also took care of the coaching team. They were available for coaching conversations with members of the team and they set up regular meetings for the coaches to share their ideas and concerns, providing tea and doughnuts as a thank you. Trevor is very clear that the sustainability and success of coaching was in no small part due to the leadership provided by Sue and Julie. He regarded them as key drivers of the programme, essentially because they led from the front, organised further training, liaised with members of the senior team and kept morale buoyant when the going got tough. He reflected, 'Beware of taking coaches for granted. They need to be recognised'.

Julie endorsed this view and made some telling points about the management of coaching in a large comprehensive school:

– coaches need line managers

– the school needs to develop a climate in which all leaders understand the value of coaching and are supportive of it

– time is needed for ongoing training for the coaches and, for example, for video coaching conversations.

 Case study: Bognor Regis Community College – the science department

A year after coming out of special measures, a short-term plan had been established to support the science department by the head of department, a senior team member and the local authority science adviser. The plan had the following objectives:

• to improve the practice in the science department
• to make lessons fun for students
• to further develop AfL strategies
• to celebrate improvements in teaching and learning and thus raise staff morale
• to improve teachers' planning
• to enable students to feel positive about their progress in science.

(Continued)

(Continued)

The plan included, as one of its actions, the appointment of a coach for each member of the department, including temporary staff. The intention was that the coaches would work alongside the teachers to plan lessons for specific groups of children that were identified by the teachers as posing significant challenges.

A joint planning meeting was held between the coaches and the science teachers at the start of the term. This was a difficult situation that carried considerable risks. Nevertheless by the end of the meeting it was clear that the coaches and members of the department had begun to build rapport and requests were made by department members to be paired with specific coaches.

As the initiative got under way, joint planning between coaches and coachees did indeed take place but this was in practice only a small part of the collaborative work that was undertaken. For example, the coaches offered their science colleagues Inset sessions that were based on the school's good practice in the development of literacy for learning. This training, in the opinion of the school's lead literacy coach, was a key to the success of the project because it provided some tools that the teachers could use to help their students to talk and write more effectively about their science – an issue that the scientists had recognised from the outset – and it was something that did not encroach directly on their expertise as *science* teachers.

In addition, there were one-to-one coaching conversations to support the implementation of the work on literacy and some partnerships focused on active engagement strategies, classroom management and dealing with 'stuck' pupils. In some cases the coaches provided in-class support and others were present in the science corridors at lesson changeovers to help to settle the children. In effect, the coaches responded to the needs of the science teachers as they emerged and did so positively, non-judgementally and with empathy.

At the outset, it was the coaches who provided the positive energy and unfailing optimism that is needed for things to improve, but as the process continued it became clear to Julie Woodward that the science team was developing what she called 'the Dunkirk spirit'. They were supporting each other, sharing ideas about teaching and class management and, in doing so, the morale of the department was rising. Over the period of the initiative, the department won the school's weekly prize for sharing innovative ideas for teaching on three occasions, and this undoubtedly contributed to the teachers feeling good about themselves and their work.

At the end of term, Sue Bond summed up the benefits of the programme, as she saw them, as follows:

- it had helped the science teachers to refocus their energies on teaching and learning
- the morale of the department had improved
- sharing ideas and talking about teaching and learning had become the norm.

The lead coaches prepared a report in which they included the following quantitative data that was helpful in evaluating the impact of the initiative:

- staff absences declined in the department by over 60% during the term
- the department's use of the school's on-call system dropped by over 30% during the term, compared with the previous four months
- the teachers massively increased their use of key learning and teaching strategies.

Ingredients of good teaching and learning	Increase during initiative (%)
Good subject knowledge displayed	20
Planning enabling learning	20
Sharing AfL targets with students	40
Sharing format of lessons (**S**tarter, **L**earning objectives, **A**ctvities, **P**lenary = SLAP)	63
Including a relevant starter activity	34
Addressing learning style preferences – visual, auditory and kinaesthetic (VAK)	100
Meeting the needs of different learners	48
An appropriate range of activities	80
Use of plenaries and mini plenaries	60
Sharing of success criteria	47
Independent and collaborative work by students	52
Use of formative feedback	80
Effective questioning	92
Peer assessment undertaken by students	40
Evidence of pace and challenge	52
A positive learning environment was created	13
Evidence of a good climate for learning, expectations and positive relationships	30
Use of specific literacy strategies	55
Evidence of setting targets for the next stage of learning	73
Active engagement of students	60

Figure 7.2 Ingredients of good teaching and learning

Figure 7.2 summarises these improvements and is based on the school's walk-through monitoring of the department before and towards the end of the initiative. In addition, qualitative data was obtained from interviews with teachers and students. Some of the most telling comments are included below:

Science staff

- The coaches have had a huge impact in terms of support.

- It has been nice to know that [coach] was interested in what I was doing and was there if I needed her.

- Meeting with the coaches has given me the confidence to develop new ideas.

- I think it was a fantastic idea. It definitely raised morale.

- People are sharing and talking about teaching again.

Students

- Our teacher has changed and become nicer.

- Our teacher jokes with us now.

- We do experiments every day! It's well good.

 Case study: Bognor Regis Community College – Ian's story

Ian is an experienced science teacher who, by his own admission, had been feeling isolated in his classroom and adrift from the rest of the department in the lower school. He had been observed teaching during one of the walk-through monitoring periods and the change in his practice was extraordinary. The students were actively engaged in their learning by, for example, playing a starter game that was designed to tease out definitions of scientific terms, and Ian was clearly relaxed and enjoying his teaching once more.

When Ian was interviewed at the end of the term to find out what he thought about the science coaching initiative, he explained that he had been considering for some time the possibility of adapting the science department's thinking frames, in the light of the school's training on AfL. The assistant headteacher, with a responsibility for the development of literacy strategies, had introduced the notion of PEE (*P*oint, *E*vidence, *E*xplain) as a way of helping to structure sentences but Ian had struggled to apply this to science. A coaching session with Julie had resulted in the idea of organising thinking into four sections – topic, development, support and conclusion – and this seemed to work. He also took the idea of 'caterpillars' from INSET, provided as part of the science coaching, and used it successfully to help children to develop their scientific explanations. He explained that the coaching dialogue had helped to clarify his thinking and that this literacy work with his year 7 classes had resulted in children of all abilities exceeding their targets. He was now considering how to differentiate more effectively in the classroom and was pondering the value of using children's literacy levels to group them for learning in science.

In summing up, he remarked, 'It's improved my teaching. It's improved my quality of life in general. I'm much happier'.

(Continued)

(Continued)

And what did his students think? They had certainly seen a change and had commented in the feedback:

> 'Our teacher is wicked – great!'
> 'It's fun.'
> 'We've had loads of great lessons.'

 Question for reflection and discussion

Is there any good practice described in this chapter that could be adapted to your context?

 Summary

With the right leadership, which can clearly come from different places in the organisation, teachers in challenging schools can be persuaded to see coaching as a positive way of addressing their immediate professional needs. However, it is clear that the whole-hearted and long-term support of senior leadership is needed for coaching to be accepted and to become a significant factor in school improvement.

Schools, particularly when under the pressure of regular inspection visits, need to identify key staff who will drive the coaching initiative and who will provide good leadership and management of the coaching team.

It is important to ensure that the coaches develop their confidence and skills by working with each other, after their initial training, before they take on the job of supporting their colleagues across the school.

Ongoing training will be needed for the coaches as well as opportunities for them to meet to discuss their work and to be coached.

Some means will need to be found to measure the impact of coaching on teaching and learning. This issue is explored in more detail in Chapter 10.

Be prepared to allow the coaching model in the school to change, or to 'mutate', as the climate in the school and the needs of the staff change.

The first steps for school leaders

This chapter is of particular interest to school leaders and will consider:

- how to carry out a whole-school CPD audit
- how to identify and train potential coaches
- how to establish whole-school coaching protocols.

As we move towards a more personalised learning experience for pupils, it is important that we adopt a similar philosophy for the CPD needs of our staff. To continue to be effective teachers in the classroom, we need to ensure that our own CPD needs are met. At the moment there is a general move away from seeing CPD as an entitlement, to a view that CPD is the personal responsibility of all staff. This requires a shift away from the view that CPD is all about 'going on a course' and towards a view of CPD as a continuous, sustained and active process, which involves teachers developing each other from the huge range of skills and expertise that already exists in any school. In this sense, coaching is the purest form of staff development and should form the basis of a varied and comprehensive CPD programme within a school.

 Question for reflection and discussion

Does your school offer its staff a varied and personalised diet of CPD activities?

As school leaders, it is important to have a very clear insight into the CPD needs of our staff and we recommend surveying staff CPD needs on a regular basis, using a questionnaire (see Figure 8.1 for an example).

CPD activity	How well used is this type of CPD?				I would like to be offered more opportunities for this type of activity
Subject _____	Very good	Good	OK	Poor	
Attending external course/event					
Closure day: external trainer (whole school)					
Closure day: sharing of staff expertise					
Closure day: working within faculties/ departments					
Sharing expertise					
Self-evaluation					
Observing colleagues at work					
Collaborative planning, teaching and review					
Reading literature					
Mentoring/coaching with feedback on performance					
Working with colleagues from other schools as part of a project					
Working with colleagues from other schools as part of a network					
Developing resources with colleagues					
Shadowing colleagues					
Sharing good practice at meetings					
Working with the AIS/consultants in schools					
Carrying out small-scale research					
Working alongside an 'expert'					
Write your additional comments here:					

Figure 8.1   CPD staff questionnaire

 Photocopiable:
The Coaching Toolkit © Shaun Allison and Michael Harbour, 2009 (SAGE)

Case study: Littlehampton Community School – conducting a CPD audit

The following questionnaires (Figure 8.2 and Figure 8.3) were completed at Littlehampton Community School.

CPD activity	Rating
Attending external course/event	3.0
Self-evaluation	2.6
Mentoring/coaching with feedback on performance	2.6
Closure day: external speaker (whole school)	2.6
Collaborative planning, teaching and review	2.6
Observing colleagues at work	2.5
Developing resources with colleagues	2.4
Reading literature	2.3
Sharing good practice at meetings	2.3
Closure day: working within faculties/departments	2.3
Sharing expertise	2.2
Working with colleagues from other schools as part of a network	2.2
Working alongside an 'expert'	2.1
Working with colleagues from other schools as part of a project	2.1
Closure day: sharing of LCS staff expertise	2.1
Carrying out small-scale research	1.9
Working with the AIS/consultants in schools	1.9
Shadowing colleagues	1.8

4 = very good
3 = good
2 = okay
1 = poor

Figure 8.2   CPD activities rated by how well they were being used at Littlehampton

CPD activity	More opps (%)
Developing resources with colleagues	31.9
Closure day: working within faculties/departments	31.9
Attending external course/event	29.8
Sharing expertise	27.7
Closure day: sharing of LCS staff expertise	27.7
Collaborative planning, teaching and review	23.4
Mentoring/coaching with feedback on performance	21.3
Working with colleagues from other schools as part of a project	21.3
Observing colleagues at work	17.0
Working with colleagues from other schools as part of a network	17.0
Shadowing colleagues	17.0
Working alongside an 'expert'	14.9
Carrying out small-scale research	12.8
Sharing good practice at meetings	10.6
Reading literature	8.5
Working with the AIS/consultants in schools	8.5
Self-evaluation	4.3
Closure day: external speaker (whole school)	4.3

Figure 8.3   CPD activities rated by the percentage of staff that wanted more opportunities to engage in that type of CPD

(Continued)

(Continued)

Some interesting comments made by staff about their CPD included the following:

- 'I feel that we have some excellent expertise in school and need more opportunity to share this between colleagues.'
- 'I think that working with other schools who exhibit best practice in your subject is a useful strategy for improving your own.'
- 'I would really like cross-school observations to see departments and classes across the county.'
- 'Sitting in the hall all day, being talked at, is generally viewed as a waste of precious time. Even if the speakers are good, it is often repetitive. Could at least some of them be optional for those who wish to focus on that aspect?'
- 'Much more shared planning and observation of other staff would be excellent as would time to plan within faculties.'
- 'I would like more opportunity to observe and be observed by my peers – in a non-judgemental way.'

It is a good idea then to offer a range of CPD activities that allow staff to develop their own teaching skills, from the existing good practice of their colleagues. The 'one size fits all' approach does not work, so avoid having everyone sit in the hall for a day being spoken to by an external speaker. We suggest that good CPD should involve:

- sharing existing expertise with colleagues

- observing and being observed by peers – in a non-judgemental way

- planning collaboratively (within or across departments)

- developing resources with colleagues.

These are all issues that can be addressed by coaching. The questionnaire is a useful resource, as it can give a very clear indication of whether the climate within a school is right for coaching.

It is very important to be clear about what you want to achieve from coaching. When we start working with a school on coaching, it soon becomes clear that there is a large number of excellent teachers within the school, many of whom have the capacity to develop others. In essence, this is the objective of coaching – to use the expertise that already exists within the school to draw out and develop the skills of other teachers. This is not a new idea – and it certainly isn't rocket science. What we need to do, at every possible opportunity, is to provide opportunities for colleagues to talk to each other and work with each other on aspects of teaching and learning.

Once you are clear about what you want coaching to do for you, consider what would be the most appropriate coaching model for your school. For example:

- a small group of teaching and learning coaches to work with colleagues on an issue of their choice

- developing coaching skills with the whole staff

- using specialist coaches – coaches who develop the practice of others in a particular area, for example AfL or facilitating the achievement of specific performance management targets

- coaching for a specific group such as middle leaders.

In terms of getting coaching under way, schools could start by identifying the teachers who they know are good, consistent practitioners and who also demonstrate many of the skills that are important for coaching. This poses a couple of interesting questions. Firstly, does a coach need to be a good teacher? The coaching purists would argue not, due to the fact that coaching is about drawing out the solutions to somebody's issues by listening and effective questioning. It does not require the coach to have all the answers and should not involve the coach telling the coachee what to do. We take a far more pragmatic view of this and believe that it depends very much on the approach to coaching that you are adopting. If you are setting up a small team of coaches to work alongside colleagues then, from a credibility point of view, they need to be sound practitioners. Is a teacher who is struggling with behaviour management really going to be keen to be coached by somebody who regularly has their students swinging from the light fittings? Probably not! On the other hand, if you are expecting all of your staff to adopt a coaching approach, then of course this will not be an issue. We are rapidly coming to the conclusion that there are few hard and fast rules for coaching. You do what works for your institution and your context.

One starting point would be to have a small group of trained coaches. So, how are the coaches identified? Your school will hold a wealth of information about the features of teaching and learning and the qualities of the teachers themselves. This will include feedback from formal lesson observations, outcomes of informal conversations between teachers and their heads of departments, records of performance management interviews, feedback from department and year monitoring walk-throughs (brief monitoring visits to classrooms) and anecdotal evidence from colleagues who have observed each other teach or who may have done some team teaching together. Some schools even hold information about observed lessons on a central database.

A useful starting point might be for teachers to audit their skills, using a tool such as the Teaching Audit (see this book's accompanying website) or the National Strategy questionnaire (see Pedagogy and Practice: *Teaching and Learning in Secondary Schools: Leadership Guide* 5 using the Teaching and learning evaluation schedule (DfES, 2004). This approach will provide the school with a 'directory of good practice' and will, of course, be useful in the identification of individuals who possess a good range of pedagogy. It could also be helpful in focusing whole-school training needs or indeed the areas of practice that individuals wish to work on in their coaching partnerships.

Whatever the sources of the information, someone will need to use it to take a hard look both at the technical capabilities of the teachers and at their interpersonal qualities, in order to identify the potential of colleagues to act as coaches. In many large secondary schools, the person well placed to do this is the training manager/CPD co-ordinator because he or she will probably know more about the teachers than any other individual in the school. Alternatively, the senior team may decide to pool their knowledge or to invite curriculum leaders to put forward the names of colleagues in their departments who have already had an impact on the teaching of others.

Using one of these routes you will identify potential coaches who should then be invited to attend training in order to find out more about coaching and to consider whether they would wish to commit to playing a key role in the development of the school's coaching programme (see Chapter 9 for an outline of an initial training day). Of course, the training experience will be useful in helping you to decide which of your colleagues have the necessary qualities and skills to become effective coaches. Sometimes the training identifies colleagues who are temperamentally not suited to coaching, because they simply cannot overcome the desire to tell others what to do!

Following the training, it will be useful for the coaches to carry on practising their skills on each other by conducting mutual lesson observations, giving non-judgemental feedback (as described in Chapter 3) and conducting coaching conversations to develop further the four key skills (listening, reflecting, clarifying and questioning). In the meantime the school will need to put in place the other essentials – a coaching protocol (see Chapter 9) and mechanisms for identifying the needs of coachees and for matching coachee to coach.

The alternative approach to having a group of trained coaches is to have the whole staff undergo some kind of coaching training. The obvious advantage to this is that you then have a huge pool of potential coaches to draw from. If all the staff have undergone some basic coaching training, then colleagues are able to support each other in this way.

 Case study: Littlehampton Community School – training a group of coaches

At Littlehampton, our initial approach with coaching was to have a small group of trained coaches. We did this for a number of reasons. Firstly, and probably most importantly, was the fact that coaching was new to us, so we wanted to start small. This would then allow us to monitor, evaluate and review the process closely. The other issue was that of training the staff. It would be easier to train a small group in the skills of coaching than the whole staff – which in our case was 140! The idea was that these coaches would then offer their services to colleagues, who would then opt to work with one of the coaches on an issue of their choice.

Initially, all the potential coaches knew was that they were going to be involved in coaching. They didn't really know what it was, how they would do it and how it would work. The group was split in two and a day was spent with each half delivering the following programme:

Objectives

- To understand the rationale behind coaching and the differences between coaching and mentoring
- To explore some of the live issues in developing coaching at Littlehampton
- To make the skills of coaching explicit, to use coaching skills and to experience the benefits of coaching

(Continued)

(Continued)

Programme for the day

- Exploring our own beliefs about learning and teaching
- Coaching and mentoring: the rationale, definitions and benefits
- Live issues for setting up coaching at Littlehampton
- Skills for coaching
- Putting the skills into practice – trying out coaching on each other by working in trios
- The next steps – how we implement coaching at Littlehampton

The days were a great success. The coaches really bonded as a group and were beginning to get a clear picture about what coaching was and the part they could play in making it a success at Littlehampton.

Establishing protocols

Once you have decided what you want to achieve from coaching at your school, you need to consider how you are going to do it. It is worth spending some time thinking through some protocols, and getting them in place, before you start any coaching. This is particularly the case if you are planning some one-to-one coaching conversations. Consider the following questions:

- What are our principles of coaching?

- What protocols will we work to?

- How will these protocols be established?

- What will a coaching relationship look like in our school?

As we discussed in Chapter 3, ground rules for coaching are important because they clarify the parameters within which you are working. There are broadly two ways of establishing these protocols – top down or bottom up. For the top-down approach, those setting up the coaching programme decide on a set of protocols and present them to the staff. They are told that this is the way the school thinks coaching should work and that these are the protocols that have been established. When we first started along the journey of coaching, this was the approach that we took. The protocol that we used is similar to Figure 8.5.

When entering into a coaching relationship, both the coach and the coachee should be asked to read and sign the document. Although this may seem rather formal, it simply serves to outline what the process would involve and how it would work. It is important that everything is transparent and open and, by doing this, people feel comfortable enough to engage with the process. The other advantage of this approach is that it acts as a prompt, generating discussion on what coaching is all about.

Similarly, it is important to explain that lesson observation, if part of the coaching process, should not be judgemental.

Dear _____

We are currently in the process of setting up a teaching and learning coaching programme at _____ School. The principles of this are very simple – good, effective and reflective classroom practitioners are trained in the skills of coaching to work alongside other colleagues, with a view to drawing out and developing good practice.

We very much appreciate the work that you do at _____ School and would like to ask you to consider being a part of the programme – as a coach. This would involve the following:

- attending a one-day training course on coaching skills
- developing these coaching skills further, by practising on each other in pairs, for the rest of this academic year – before going 'live'
- attending a further one-day training course towards the end of the summer term to review progress and to plan for the year ahead
- starting to work with a colleague (who has volunteered for the programme) in a coaching pair from _____.

The plan is to have ____ coaches trained and in place by _____, with a view to training a further ____ by _____. The Department for Children, Schools and Families (DCSF) recognises that coaching is an essential skill for potential school leaders, as well as one of the key criteria for passing through the performance thresholds. So from the point of view of your own professional development, being involved in this programme would be invaluable.

I would be really grateful if you would contact me before the end of this week so that we can make an appointment for early next half-term to discuss your involvement in this programme.

I look forward to chatting with you soon.

Regards

(Coaching Co-ordinator)

Figure 8.4 Sample coach invite letter

 Photocopiable:

1 The objective of peer coaching is to improve the quality of teaching by developing and sharing good practice. It is a collaborative process.

2 Colleagues have been identified who are willing to share their practice and to support the development of teaching and classroom management skills in others. In the process, they too will develop their skills.

3 Teachers may volunteer to work in coaching partnerships.

4 No one will enter a coaching relationship without the agreement of both parties.

5 Coaches are willing to:

- offer coaching in lesson planning, classroom management and learning and teaching strategies
- observe the teaching of others and be observed themselves
- give detailed, positive feedback about the lessons which they observe
- demonstrate particular teaching skills and strategies
- work alongside colleagues in the classroom to an agreed plan
- contribute to the school's professional development programme.

6 Coaching partnerships will adhere to the following code of conduct:

- The focus of their work will be the sharing and development of good practice.
- The desired outcomes of the coaching partnership will be mutually agreed.
- Discussions will be confidential.
- The dates and times of any classroom visits will be negotiated.
- Verbal and written feedback as a result of a classroom visit will be given within five working days of the visit.
- All conversations about the teaching will take place in private and in a relaxed but professional atmosphere.
- Any lesson observation notes will remain the property of the teacher.
- It is recommended that the partners each keep a reflective log. In addition, each partnership will keep a brief, confidential written record of the work that is mutually agreed.
- The decision to commit to further action or to change practice is the prerogative of the individual.

Signed:_____

_____

Date: _____

Figure 8.5 Protocol for peer coaching

 Photocopiable:

The alternative approach to setting protocols is to do it from the bottom up, allowing the staff to decide what the protocols would be. This is an important process for the staff to go through, as it will achieve two objectives:

1   Demystifying coaching – by coming up with the protocols themselves, staff are able to work through some of the issues that they might otherwise have had with it.

2   Ownership – by coming up with the protocols themselves, the staff would be clear that this is not something being done to them, but in fact is a process over which they have control.

 Case study: Littlehampton Community School – establishing protocols

At Littlehampton, establishing protocols was done very simply during a coaching Inset day. Once staff had been introduced to the idea of coaching and had the opportunity to try it out, they were then asked to consider two questions:

1   How would you want coaching to work at our school?
2   How would you like to see coaching developed at our school?

In response to the first question, which in a sense was asking the staff to come up with their own set of protocols for coaching, they had the following suggestions:

- clear ground rules set
- trust
- respect
- non-judgemental
- friendship
- no paper
- a mutual interest
- confidentiality
- reliability.

The staff response to this question was quite significant. It was evident that the teachers wanted the process to be clear and transparent, but also that the coaching pairing had to be right. It had to be one built on mutual trust and respect, as well as being non-judgemental and confidential. The climate was therefore right for peer coaching at our school, and the staff were ready to move on with it.

The responses to the second question gave the following useful suggestions for establishing coaching within a school:

- Set up coaching partnerships for all staff.
- Volunteer for coaching – marrying up coaches and coachees – both parties must be happy with choices to enable a successful partnership.
- Use informal, non-judgemental coaching.
- Allow it to develop through staff being able to chat informally about an area or problem.
- Promote it as a norm – perhaps most staff could have a 'named' coach who they can speak with should they wish. They *don't have to* but they *can*.

(Continued)

(Continued)

- Create a culture of trust and positivity.
- Give staff the opportunity to observe their peers.
- Make all staff aware of what coaching is and that it can be very specific to their needs.
- Ensure staff realise that it is non-judgemental and confidential.
- Give new and existing staff the opportunity to choose their coach to ensure good relationships, trust and respect.
- Focus on making it a sharing experience. Lots of classroom teachers are quite good at this already – sometimes 'responsibility' gives people a front that discourages sharing. They sometimes hide behind the appearance of 'coping' or 'knowing better'.

This process was hugely significant. It was interesting to see that many of the suggestions were far more ambitious than would have been otherwise suggested. For example, the notion of allocating everybody a coach was not something that we had contemplated. Although this is very positive and affirming it may not have been the right thing to do. Coaching will only work if the person wants to be coached and if that person has some control over whom she or he will work with. To allocate everybody a coach, whether they want it or not, goes against these two important premises. The suggestion that people should volunteer to coach and be coached was more in line with the way successful coaching develops. What was coming through quite strongly was the notion that people saw this as a positive process and that they were interested.

If you are starting from scratch in terms of setting up coaching as a whole-school process, we would almost certainly suggest the bottom-up approach to establishing coaching protocols. Why?

- It gives staff a sense of ownership over the process – it is something that they are in control of and it is not something that is being done to them.

- It allows staff to air and address their concerns over the process.

As a result, they are far more likely to engage in coaching.

 Case study: Clarendon College, Trowbridge, Wiltshire

A mixed comprehensive school in the south of England with approximately 1300 students on roll.

Introduction

The role of teacher coach was established at Clarendon College and two full-time teachers took it on following a selection process that included a lesson observation, that could take place at any time over two weeks, and then an

(Continued)

(Continued)

interview discussing various fictional coaching scenarios. After the first year, these two teachers left the school and therefore the role was available again. Katie Morgan became one of two teacher coaches and the roles have been developing since then.

Coaching is non-judgemental and confidential, and is an important part of the CPD process within the college. Although it has to be evaluated and reported on to senior leadership, they are unaware of who has been coached. Evaluations are kept anonymous and feedback is used to improve what is offered.

Process

Teacher coaches are available for all staff to use throughout the year – it is not simply a process for teachers who are experiencing difficulties or underperforming. Currently, all NQTs and second-year teachers go through the coaching process as part of their school induction support and services are also offered to all staff, including unqualified teachers and classroom supervisors. A group of ten teachers who are currently on the Clarendon Middle Leadership Course have been worked with this year, the intention being that they recommend coaching to colleagues they line manage.

Five lessons are identified for coaching over a two-week timetable. One of these lessons is used for a meeting with the line manager and the other four are for lesson observations and feedback sessions. An observation is arranged and the coach and coachee agree on one or two areas to concentrate on. The feedback session takes place a couple of days after the observation and is an informal conversation about the lesson and how to move the teacher forward. Teachers can then decide if they would like the coach to return to observe them with the same class or a different class after an agreed period of time. Some teachers choose to have only one session whereas others use the coaches on a regular basis throughout the year.

Impact

The process has been carried out with approximately 20 teachers so far this year and initial feedback has been very positive. Evaluations from last year have shown that coaching has made a significant contribution to raising standards of teaching and learning within the college and this has had an impact on lesson observations using Ofsted-style gradings.

Summary

It is important to think carefully about what you want coaching to achieve in your school and to carry out a CPD audit to determine where coaching may already be happening and where there may be gaps in provision.

Deciding on the approach that is right for your school is also vital as there is no 'one size fits all' approach to coaching – it has to be right for your context. To ensure that you are using the right approach, it is important to think carefully about who to train initially in the skills of coaching and how you will do it. Be clear about how you will set up coaching protocols – top down or bottom up – and ensure that these protocols are adhered to by staff.

Electronic resources

Go to www.sagepub.co.uk/allison for electronic resources for this chapter

Teaching audit

Procedures for peer coaching

CPD staff questionnaire

Protocol for peer coaching

Sample coach invite letter

Further reading

Fleming, I. and Taylor, A. (1998) *The Coaching Pocketbook.* Alresford: Management Pocketbooks.

Establishing peer coaching across the school

This chapter is of particular interest to school leaders and will consider:

- issues that arise regarding coaching and how to deal with them
- selling the idea of coaching to the whole school
- identifying the needs of coachees and matching them with a coach
- meeting the needs of the coaches.

So, you have decided that you are going to use coaching to develop the quality of teaching and learning at your school. You are clear about the purpose of coaching and what you want it to do. You may have some trained coaches in place – all ready to go. You may even have had the whole staff trained. You have also developed some agreed protocols for coaching. The difficult bit is getting staff to subscribe to coaching and then doing it. Only then will it actually begin to have any impact. This chapter will examine how to do that.

There are many potential pitfalls with coaching. Some of these can be anticipated and addressed, in order to avoid them becoming an impediment to developing coaching in your school. Some of the issues or questions that staff may have regarding coaching are outlined below, along with some possible ways to address them.

Do I get paid for coaching?

Coaching is a skill that we should all be developing in order to support and develop our colleagues. Clearly, this will be happening to different degrees with different people. For example, a subject leader or an AST will be using coaching skills to a greater degree than a class teacher who is informally supporting a colleague – but they will all be using the skills. The underlying principle is that it is just a decent way of working for all of us and is therefore not something we would be paid for.

Where do I find the time to coach?

When a school has established a real culture of coaching, this will not be an issue. Coaching will not be seen as something separate to the other things that we do – it will become a part of how we do it. So, the conversation over the coffee machine, the development activity in a department meeting, or the whole-staff meeting will all contain an element of coaching. When a more formal arrangement is required, for example when teacher A wants to work with teacher B in a coaching relationship to develop her AfL work, then schools can be creative to accommodate this. You could try turning Inset days into CPD twilight sessions and have staff attend six throughout the year, to get the two disaggregated days off school. However, if teachers are engaged in some coaching work, then they need only attend say four of these sessions in recognition of the work that they are putting into coaching.

A forward-thinking team in a school will remove a lot of the 'stuff' on meeting agendas to make way for coaching conversations to happen. This will be a challenge for many teams, especially those that feel that the discussion regarding the number of exercise books that need to be ordered for next year is of great pedagogical importance! In any event, coaching can be done 'on the hoof'. Practised coaches learn to have coaching conversations in chunks when necessary, with each part of the session being conducted at a different time. In these circumstances it is really useful to end each mini session with a summing up or a key question for the coachee to consider before the next meeting.

I'm doing it already

To be honest, this is probably true. When setting up coaching in schools, you will be refining many of the skills that already exist amongst staff. Coaching is not rocket science and many good teachers do it quite naturally. If this is the case, great – but how can these colleagues develop coaching skills in others? Engaging in the school's coaching programme will refine their skills and make them better placed to develop future coaches.

I have no issues to address, so I don't need it

This assumes that coaching is always about addressing a weakness. This is not the case. It can be about taking something that you already do well, and doing it better. Starting with a first cohort of staff who are trained in coaching skills and are all strong teachers with credibility amongst their peers is a strong position to build on. It gives an important message to staff that coaching could serve a purpose for everyone and is not just about targeting weak teachers.

Why not me?

When the first cohort of teachers are trained in coaching, many staff may respond by asking 'What's special about them? Why can't I do it?' – and they have a point. The approach to coaching can be adapted to give all staff some coaching training, so in theory anyone could coach anyone. People who then want to take it further, should be given the opportunity to do so.

Demystify coaching

This ties in with the point above and is key to the success of coaching in schools. A big breakthrough is made with coaching when it is presented, explained and discussed with all staff. They can then see the purpose of it and also its potential. However, this can only really happen once all staff have had the opportunity to try it out for themselves. Nevertheless, it may be worth devoting some time at a staff meeting to explaining the rationale behind coaching and initial plans before going too far. (See the initial slides in the Coaching for Performance PowerPoint presentation, included in the electronic resources for this chapter, for some ideas.)

I haven't got time for this, why can't I just tell them what to do?

A common and perfectly natural response – bearing in mind the hectic and busy ways in which schools operate. However, if this is all we ever do, then all our colleagues will do is continue to ask instead of looking to find the solutions for themselves. Coaching is about breaking the cycle of dependency, which in turn results in sustainable progress.

Why can't all staff be involved with coaching?

They can, but if it is to be successful, some planning is worthwhile. Experience has shown us that the most effective way to sell coaching to all staff, is through the staff sharing their experiences of coaching informally. Just telling colleagues that it is a good idea, is not enough. From a practical point of view, it may be worth getting a few people involved in it first of all. Following this, provide opportunities for them to tell their colleagues that it is a worthwhile and useful process and wait for it to snowball. Then provide further opportunities for all staff to be involved. A word of warning at this point – it will then seem to go very quiet on the coaching front, and you will think that it is not happening. However, if you ask people casually 'how's the coaching?', you will be surprised to hear just how much is going on. When you get to this point, you are definitely moving in the right direction, towards developing a culture of coaching.

 Question for reflection and discussion

Which of these issues will be particularly relevant to your institution? Consider the answers, in your own context, before embarking on coaching.

Just as we have argued for the value of trios in the training of a small group of coaches, so learning sets of threes can be an effective way of maintaining coaching across the staff.

One advantage of developing coaching trios is that the focus is very much on planning and sharing ideas rather than necessarily on lesson observation and feedback. This addresses a problem that was identified by Joyce and Showers in their work on peer coaching teams (1996: 12–16). They observed that:

> when teachers try to give one another feedback, collaborative activity tends to disintegrate. Peer coaches told us they found themselves slipping into 'supervisory, evaluative comments' despite their intentions to avoid them ... [Teachers] often pressured their coaches to go beyond technical feedback and give them 'the real scoop'.

Their solution was to move away from the observation and discussion format to coaching teams, which are not unlike our trios.

The other group of people who need to subscribe to the idea of coaching, if it is going to be a success in your school, is the leadership team. They need to be modelling a coaching approach when dealing with colleagues, if it is going to become a common way of working within the school. How can this be done?

- Initially, you may need to explain the rationale behind coaching to the senior leadership team (SLT). Unpacking Joyce and Showers' research (2002 and see Chapter 2) and exploring the advantages of coaching as opposed to other forms of CPD have proved to be useful starting points in some schools.

- Train the senior team in coaching skills. Suggest that they go through the initial training programme, either as a group or mixed in with other staff, depending on their availability and on the messages that they wish to send to their colleagues.

- Encourage them to attend and participate in coaching-based Inset days. You have seen at Mayfield School (Chapter 7) what a powerful message is sent to the staff when, for example, the headteacher takes a clear and visible coaching role as part of a school's CPD activity.

- Engage school leaders with National College for School Leadership (NCSL) programmes such as Leading from the Middle, Leadership Pathways and the National Professional Qualification for Headteachers, all of which use coaching as part of the training process.

 Question for reflection and discussion

To what extent does the leadership team within your school use coaching as a leadership style?

Identifying the needs of coachees

As we suggested in Chapter 8, a self-audit of teaching could be a good starting point for identifying the specific needs of teachers which could be voluntarily shared at the outset of the coaching relationship.

Some schools will have specific areas of focus that arise from their monitoring of teaching and learning. So, for example, the starting point for coaching may be AfL or the development of effective plenary opportunities in lessons. In this case, the whole staff, or a sub-group of teachers, would be expected to work on the chosen aspect of teaching and learning for a period of time and those teachers who have volunteered to engage in coaching would then use the coaching programme to develop that specific aspect of their pedagogy, whether they are advanced practitioners or not.

Subject leaders should have a clear idea about the areas for development in their staff and may be helpful in steering colleagues towards a coaching partnership. They will need to do so with tact and sensitivity.

Some schools invite teachers to engage in coaching by distributing a request for coaching form (see Figure 9.1), usually following a CPD session in which the principles and advantages of coaching are explored.

Whatever strategies are adopted to help colleagues to identify their needs as coachees, it is clear that the coaching process will not work unless the coachees are willing participants in the process and not conscripts. It is equally clear that, as the coaching relationship develops, the real targets and challenges become evident.

Coaches also have needs

As the coaching process gets under way in your school, it will become clear that the coaches will need support to fulfil their role. Common issues that confront coaches in the early stages of their work are:

- being held at a distance by a potential coachee who is feeling insecure or hesitant about taking the plunge

- difficulties in knowing how to start – how to help focus a coachee who may have a whole raft of apparent challenges to overcome

- feeling that their positive energy is being drained by colleagues whose demands seem relentless

- feeling unskilled

- feeling unable to rise to the challenge

- feeling undervalued by the school's leadership.

These are common responses in the early days. So what mechanisms does the school have to support the coaches?

Firstly, the coaches have each other as a support group which we suggest should meet every half-term in a coaching forum, perhaps under the chairmanship of the school's coaching co-ordinator, to review progress and to share helpful strategies

Name: _____

Department: _____

Date: _____

For which aspect(s) of your role would you like coaching support?

_____

_____

_____

_____

Please pass this request form to the coaching co-ordinator.

What will happen next?

- The coaching co-ordinator will talk with you confidentially to clarify the issues and to find the most suitable coaching match for you.
- A coach will then be identified for you to work with.
- You and the coach will meet to agree a focus and a plan.
- You will review the work that you do together each half-term, or earlier if the coaching process is completed in less time.
- The coaching protocol will be followed throughout the process.

Figure 9.1   Request for coaching form

 Photocopiable:
The Coaching Toolkit © Shaun Allison and Michael Harbour, 2009 (SAGE)

and the training needs of the coaches. Establish a clear protocol for the work of the forum. Commonly, it is useful to agree that the names of the coachees are never used in discussions. It may also be useful to require that the half-termly reviews between coaches and coachees have been completed before the coaching forum takes place. The reflections of all parties to the coaching process, summarised in this way, give a greater focus to the meeting.

It may be useful to organise the coaches into self-support pairs or trios tasked to provide ongoing coaching support for each other. After all, the coaches, in common with all staff, will need coaching from time to time. Alternatively, the coaching co-ordinator could provide coaching support for the coaches, either directly or by engaging the services of an external consultant. It would be usual for the ongoing training needs of the coaches to be identified through one or other of the mechanisms suggested above.

Finally, it is important that the school finds ways of acknowledging the demanding work that the coaches have undertaken.

Matching coachee and coach

Having trained coaches, established protocols for lesson observations and coaching conversations, identified the school's teaching strengths and areas for development, set up a method of inviting teachers to engage in coaching and set up a coaching forum, the school will now need to empower a colleague to match coachees with coaches in a sensitive and carefully considered manner. This person will need to enjoy the trust and confidence of teachers and will need to have a good knowledge of the staff, their strengths and weaknesses as teachers, as well as what makes them tick as people. He or she could well be the school's coaching co-ordinator or possibly a key member of the coaching team.

It is the job of this wise and highly-regarded colleague to act as go-between so that coaching partnerships are established in which the coachee and coach feel comfortable working with each other. The process will involve careful consideration of the expressed needs of the coachee. At this point the go-between will need to make a confidential approach to two or three coaches who might fit the bill in order to establish whether they would all be prepared, if chosen, to engage in a coaching relationship with that particular coachee. Armed, hopefully with their positive responses, the go-between is then able to offer the coachee some alternatives from which to choose. It is important that the coachees make real choices as this is likely to increase their commitment to the coaching relationship.

 Question for reflection and discussion

In your institution who has the knowledge and skills to match up coach and coachee?

It is worth remembering, when setting up coaching partnerships, the following words of James Flaherty (1999):

> It is dangerous for coaches to imagine that the use of any technique, however powerful, will allow them to escape engaging fully with the other person with openness, courage and curiosity. Techniques cannot replace the human heart and creativity in coaching.

Above all, the challenge for the go-between is to use emotional intelligence to identify those colleagues who are likely to strike up good rapport and to engage 'the human heart' in the coaching process.

Monitoring the coaching relationship – how long will it last?

Suggestions for monitoring and evaluating the impact of coaching, both at the individual and institutional level, are given in Chapter 10. We take the view that coaching partnerships usually need at least half a term to enable the coaching cycle to be completed and targets to be met. Following a review, towards the end of the half-term, it may be that further work needs to be done.

Summary

It is important to have a clear strategy of how you are going to sell coaching to your staff and get all members involved. This can be done by setting up coaching trios or clusters across departments and giving these groups specific tasks to carry out which will impact on the quality of teaching and learning in your school.

It is also important to dedicate time to sharing ideas about how to teach, for example by providing opportunities on training days for colleagues to discuss and demonstrate what they have been doing, and to find opportunities for recognising the work of the coaches.

By encouraging your senior team to get involved in coaching you will encourage more people to take it up, but do remember that considerable tact and sensitivity are needed when pairing up colleagues into coaching partnerships.

Electronic resources

Go to www.sagepub.co.uk/allison for electronic resources for this chapter

The coaching cycle

Coaching for performance – PowerPoint presentation

Coaching for performance – training plan

Coaching for performance – programme

Request for coaching form

10

Measuring impact

> **This chapter is of particular interest to school leaders. In it we will look at:**
>
> - why the impact of coaching on teaching and learning needs to be measured
> - the different ways in which this can be done
> - how to review how coaching is developing in your school.

If any school is to succeed, it is not enough to have a good idea and then put it into practice. A good idea is only good when it translates into positive outcomes – until then, it is just an idea. This is the case for coaching in schools. In earlier chapters, we discussed the need to establish a school's vision for coaching – what do you want it to become and what do you want it to achieve? With this in mind, it is imperative to consider how you will monitor and evaluate whether or not coaching is achieving these objectives.

> **〰 Questions for reflection and discussion**
>
> - Can coaches and coachees contribute to the review of success while maintaining confidentiality and trust?
> - What data could be gathered to infer or confirm that the coaching process has been successful?
> - What is the role of other colleagues (other than coach and coachee) in monitoring the impact of coaching?
> - What role could the children play in confirming the success of coaching?

It is worth taking some time to consider why we should monitor and evaluate the impact of any CPD activity, such as coaching, in schools.

Here are some possible reasons:

- To improve the coaching process, with a view to further improving teaching and learning.

- To improve the self-esteem of the coachees. If they feel that the process has been useful and has made a difference, they will feel better about themselves. This will undoubtedly have a positive effect on their performance.

- To provide an evidence bank for Ofsted inspections. The fact that schools are engaging in coaching will be viewed as a positive move. If it can be demonstrated that coaching is having a positive impact on teaching and learning, even better.

- To justify the process to stakeholders. It is highly likely that coaching will draw on the school's resources. It will be easier to justify this to stakeholders such as the governing body if positive outcomes can be identified.

- To grow and develop coaching. Once reluctant colleagues see that it works, they may be more likely to engage with coaching.

However, the process of monitoring and evaluating the impact of coaching is fraught with difficulties. It could be argued that it goes against the whole principle of coaching. Firstly, coaching is meant to be a confidential and non-judgemental process. As soon as you start measuring the effectiveness of it, these principles could be compromised. Secondly, coaching is just one of many interventions that could be having an impact on teaching and learning. There will be many other variables involved, for example other discussions with colleagues, reading an article in a journal, own self-reflection, a discussion at a staff or department meeting and so on. It is very difficult to draw a direct link between an improvement in the quality of teaching and learning and any coaching that the teacher may have engaged in. These two issues can be addressed by considering what can be measured to evaluate impact and how this can be done.

Feedback from coachees

At the outset of the coaching process, some kind of self-analysis may have been carried out by the coachees. This will have been used to establish how happy they are with a particular aspect of their job. Examples may include:

Job performance pie

Colleagues are asked to draw a pie chart that includes the main aspects of their role, or the main parts of their role that they are interested in addressing by coaching. The size of each segment, relates to their level of satisfaction with this part of their role. Clearly, the person represented in Figure 10.1 is equally satisfied with each part of their role! However, if this process is carried out at the beginning and at the end of the coaching process, then one might expect to see an increase in the size of the segment which relates to the focus of the coaching.

Job satisfaction chart

Working on a similar principle, a chart or graph could be used to measure how satisfied a colleague is with the different aspects of their work. This can be used at the start of the coaching process and again at the end. Comparisons can then be made and progress measured. The advantage of the faces included in Figure 10.2 is

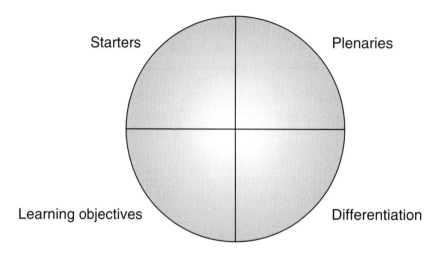

Figure 10.1   Job performance pie

Aspect of teaching	☹	😐	☐
Starters			✓
Plenaries	✓		
Learning objectives		✓	
Differentiation	✓		

Figure 10.2   Job satisfaction chart

that they are not as threatening as a numerical value. The chart is concerned with how people feel about themselves. However, from an analytical point of view, there is nothing to stop these being turned into numerical values, making a quantitative analysis of the impact possible.

A star diagram can also be used for coaching purposes. The example in Figure 10.3 focuses on the criteria for a 'good' lesson. Teachers are encouraged to assess themselves along each of the five spines, on a three-point grading system. They can then join each of the five points to obtain a visual representation of their own performance.

Questionnaire

Another way to get qualitative information from the coachee is by way of a simple questionnaire. Although not as easy to anaylse in a numerical way, it will certainly give feedback on the process. Some questions to consider include:

- Has the coaching process been useful? Why?

- What have been the main learning points for you from the process?

- How has your practice changed as a result?

Figure 10.3 'Good' lesson star diagram

- What has been the impact of this change on the learning of your students?

- What are your next steps?

- How else can we continue to develop coaching at school? What changes should we introduce for next year?

The last question is very important. Colleagues who have been coached often have very good ideas about how to move coaching on in a school.

Coaching log

In Chapter 8, it was suggested that it is good practice for both the coach and the coachee to keep a reflective coaching log that will enable them to focus further conversations and to record the progress of the coachee against his or her self-determined targets. This log will provide evidence of progress over time. It is useful, perhaps every half-term, to devote a coaching conversation to reviewing progress. The coach will need to ask good questions to elicit the coachee's realistic self-review and to avoid negative self-talk. Any notes that are made in this meeting should be agreed and should remain the property of the coachee (see Figure. 10.4 for an example of a coaching review template).

Coaching review

Date and time	Action taken (What have you done differently? What steps have you taken?)	What is the evidence of success? (What have been the outcomes for you and for the students?)	What next? (Have you any targets for the next steps?)

Signed: _____ (Coachee) _____ (Coach)

Figure 10.4   Coaching review template

 Photocopiable:
The Coaching Toolkit © Shaun Allison and Michael Harbour, 2009 (SAGE)

However, if coaching is used positively by a teacher to support the achievement of a performance management target, the teacher may choose to use evidence from the coaching log, corroborated by, for example, a lesson observation or data on student attainment, to show that he or she has achieved that particular target. There would be nothing to prevent the headteacher from totalling the number of instances when a target was met with the support of coaching, when reading the performance management summaries. This collection of data clearly would not breach any confidences.

Feedback from coaches

We now come to the vexed question: what, if anything, from a coaching review conversation could be shared with other colleagues? We take the view that the details of the conversation should remain confidential but that target areas could be described (for example, 'work on plenaries') and outcomes could be evaluated. This could be shared with the school's coaching co-ordinator, perhaps each half-term. We feel that such an approach would need the full agreement of both the coach and coachee and that any statement of progress should be jointly written or agreed.

Feedback from students

It is probably fairly accurate to assume that most schools have some kind of 'student voice' process in place. When it is most effective, student voice is used to get feedback from students on their own classroom experiences and their view on what good teaching is and how this helps their learning. If a school is engaging in specialist coaching, for example in the development of AfL, it would seem sensible to question the student voice panel on this topic. Clearly, the questions would need to be carefully phrased, but this would give honest and direct feedback on whether or not the coaching in that area is having any impact.

This approach was adopted by John McKee, an Assistant Headteacher working in Brighton. John has been using coaching to embed AfL practice into teaching and learning at his school. He then used a student questionnaire to measure the impact of the coaching on the learning experiences of the students. The questionnaire John used was based on one that was developed by Tracy Smith, Deputy Headteacher at Seven Kings High School in Ilford, Essex (see Figure 10.5). It is easy to see how such a strategy could be used before and after coaching in order to monitor the impact. The questionnaire could also be adapted, for other aspects of teaching and learning.

The quality of teaching and learning

As a part of the school self-evaluation process, schools should have a system in place to measure the quality of teaching and learning. This may include full-lesson observations, lesson 'walk-throughs' (where a number of lessons are visited in one period), student work scrutiny and subject leader interviews. Clearly, these processes should also provide evidence for the impact of coaching on teaching and learning.

We will listen to you

How do you learn?

At the moment, we are carrying out some research about how students at our school learn.

We are developing ways to help you improve your learning. This is called Assessment for Learning and is a major part of the work of the school. In order to help us develop this work, we need to know what you think about some of the things that happen in lessons.

We will be taking your responses seriously so please try to answer as sensibly and honestly as possible. Please think carefully about your responses to the questions – they only require you to put a tick or a cross in the relevant box.

The questionnaire is confidential – all we want to know is your year group and whether you are male or female.

Thank you for your help with this.

Instructions

- The first three columns ask whether or not a particular practice happens. The other column is about your preferences.
- Tick one box in the first three columns. Then tick or cross the last column to indicate whether you would like this to happen or not.
- After completing the questionnaire, hand it back to your tutor.

Year group	

Male	
Female	

(Continued)

(Continued)

When teachers ask you **questions in** class do they:

	Yes	No	Sometimes	Preferred/not preferred
Allow thinking time before expecting an answer				
Allow you to explore the answers in pairs before expecting an answer				
Use a no-hands-up approach				
Use wrong answers to develop your understanding of a topic				
Ask different types of questions that require different types of answers (e.g. one-word answers, extended answers, answers about your thoughts and ideas)				
Ask 'big' questions that you need to think about or discuss with a partner before answering				
Follow up one question with another				
Allow time for you to ask questions				

When teachers **assess** your work do they:

	Yes	No	Sometimes	Preferred/not preferred
Use a system that tells you how much you have understood about the lesson (e.g. traffic lights, smiley faces)				
Give you detailed explanations about what is expected				
Give you detailed explanations about what you have to do to be successful				
Give you examples of work to show you what is expected				
Show you how they have assessed your work				
Get you to mark the work of another student				
Get you to mark your own work				

(Continued)

(Continued)

When teachers **mark** your work do they:

	Yes	No	Sometimes	Preferred/ not preferred
Tell you what they are looking for when they set the work				
Tell you what you did well				
Tell you what you did badly				
Give advice about what you need to do to improve				
Give a grade				
Give targets				
Give comments				
Give an effort grade				
Ask you to act on the feedback that they have given you				
Talk to you about your work as well as give you written feedback				
Talk to you about your work instead of giving written feedback				

Thank you very much for completing the questionnaire.

Figure 10.5 Student survey

 Photocopiable:
The Coaching Toolkit © Shaun Allison and Michael Harbour, 2009 (SAGE)

Again, it is easier to make links between the coaching and the impact on teaching and learning if the coaching has had a specific focus, for example on developing the use of lesson starters.

There may be additional data available that could indicate the success in the coaching process. Perhaps a colleague has been coached in establishing positive relationships with children and clear rules and expectations in the classroom. In this case it would be appropriate to look at the data on, for example, the teacher's use of the school's formal rewards and sanctions systems. Possibly a teacher has experienced low self-esteem or stress symptoms as a result of difficulties and is reporting a more positive feeling about the job as a result of peer coaching. This could be evidenced in improved attendance by that teacher.

Student outcomes

It may be fair to assume that if coaching is being effective, then the quality of teaching and learning should improve and, as a result, so should the student outcomes. This is a somewhat simplistic assumption to make. We have already mentioned the fact that there are many other factors at play when it comes to student outcomes. With this in mind, it may be useful to focus the criteria more specifically. For example, if a teacher is being coached on improving the performance of his or her students in their GCSE Science coursework, then it may be more realistic to use the coursework scores of those students as a yardstick of success in terms of the coaching.

Attitudinal surveys

Experience has shown that coaching, if done well, will definitely improve the self-esteem and confidence of the coachee. This is difficult to measure, however a general attitudinal survey issued to staff will give you an insight into the impact of coaching. It is important to give some careful thought to what you want to find out from the survey and a quick internet search for 'teacher attitude survey' will offer guidance. For example, if a school wanted to gauge the willingness of staff to take risks and try new strategies as a result of coaching, the survey provided in Figure 10.6 could be used.

The coaching co-ordinator's role in gathering evidence of impact

To sum up, there is a range of evidence available in any school that could be useful in assessing the impact of coaching. This could include feedback from coaches and coachees on progress made, the results of formal lesson observations, data on the use of rewards and sanctions, attitudinal surveys; staff attendance

Aspect of practice	Agree strongly				Disagree strongly
I am currently enjoying my teaching					
My students enjoy my lessons					
I am a reflective practitioner					
I enjoy discussing teaching strategies with colleagues					
I tend to stick to tried and tested teaching strategies					
I want to develop new and innovative teaching strategies					
I am happy to take risks in the classroom and try things out					
I seek advice from others on how to develop my teaching					
I am able to evaluate my teaching and come up with ways to improve my teaching					

Figure 10.6   Teacher attitudinal survey

 Photocopiable:

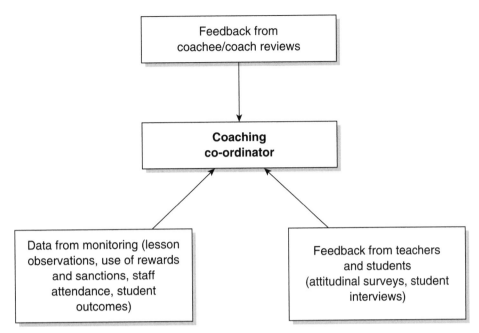

Figure 10.7   Coaching co-ordinator's role in assessing coaching

data, findings from interviews with students, and student outcomes. This information is usually held by different colleagues in a large comprehensive school. It could become the role of the coaching co-ordinator to gather this information in order to assess the impact of the coaching process (see Figure 10.7). Schools often invest a good deal of resources in setting up coaching, and so they need to develop effective mechanisms to ensure that the time and money is well used.

Reviewing how coaching is developing in your school

The more that coaching develops at a school, the more convinced we are that there are many more opportunities for coaching outside the usual pattern of two people sitting down and having a formal coaching meeting. We would advocate looking for as many opportunities as possible to use coaching as a tool for staff to support and develop each other. It is worth undertaking an audit of coaching to assess where it is happening well and developing, and where it needs to be further developed (see Figure 10.8).

This exercise could be usefully completed at the outset of planning any coaching work. However, it is also worthwhile at a later stage in the development of coaching. Having established coaching in the school, the coaching co-ordinator can sometimes feel that he or she is losing control of it. A reflective exercise such as an audit is, if nothing else, reassuring in that it highlights where coaching is happening. Of course, it also shows you where energy and resources are needed to embed coaching in all its guises.

Aspect of coaching	Embedded as a part of our practice – a strength	Developing strength	Area for further development
Peer coaching Teacher is coached by a peer on an area of their choice			
Specialist coaching Teacher is coached by a peer in a specific area, e.g. AfL			
Co-coaching Two teachers coach each other			
Team coaching Coaching occurs within a team, e.g. department, on a topic of interest to them			
Group coaching One or two teachers coach a group			
Leadership coaching Coaching is focused specifically on leadership			

Figure 10.8　A whole-school coaching audit

 Photocopiable:

Summary

On its own, none of the strategies described above will enable you to measure fully the impact of coaching or how it is developing in your school. However, when used together the strategies described they will certainly go a long way towards giving a very clear indication as to whether or not coaching is having an impact. We believe that coaching can contribute to a major cultural shift in schools – something that is difficult to measure. When coaching becomes truly embedded, staff are more receptive to change, more open to discussing what goes on in their classrooms, more willing to share aspects of their best practice and more confident about what they are doing. When this happens, then you know that coaching is really making a difference.

Electronic resources

Go to www.sagepub.co.uk/allison for electronic resources for this chapter

Coaching review template

Job satisfaction chart

Teacher attitudinal survey

Whole-school Coaching

Student survey

Suggested timeline for implementing a coaching programme

	Steps to take	Questions to consider
1	Establish within the school's senior leadership team: • a shared understanding of what coaching is • its potential in your context • a commitment to developing coaching in the school.	• What evidence is there to suggest that the school is ready to embrace coaching? • What is likely to be the focus of coaching for the school in the first year of operation? • Who will present the case for coaching to the senior team (e.g. headteacher, CPD coordinator, lead teacher(s))? (See Chapters 1 and 2 for some ideas)
2	Formulate an action plan for the introduction of coaching into the school (first year).	• What are the staff needs that coaching may help to address How do you know? • What will be the intial contexts for coaching in your school? (e.g. experienced teachers, trainee teachers, children, new teachers, all staff)? • To what extent will topics for coaching conversations be directed? • What are your success criteria for year 1? • How will you monitor and evaluate the impact of coaching? • Who will lead the initiative at the start? • Who will write the action plan? (See Chapters 8 and 10)
3	Raise staff awareness about: • what coaching is • the power of coaching to develop good practice • the plans for coaching in the school.	• How will you do this? In what forum? At what stage in the development of coaching? Who is able to 'sell' coaching to colleagues without threatening or patronising them? (See Chapters 1, 2 and 9)

(Continued)

(Continued)

	Steps to take	Questions to consider
4	**Identify teachers who have the potential to become effective coaches.**	• What criteria will you use to identify potential coaches? • Do any staff have prior experience of coaching? • Have you decided to train all staff in 'the basics'? (See Chapters 1 and 8)
5	**Train staff in the skills of coaching.**	• Who will train the staff? Over what period of time? How many staff will be trained? • To what extent will the training need to be differentiated? (See Chapter 8)
6	**Set up opportunities for colleagues to practise their coaching skills.**	• Will all the staff be able to practise coaching skills as part of their CPD? • Will coaches work with each other before 'going live' with coachees? • Do you intend to provide opportunities for coaches to be coached in the early stages of their work? (See Chapter 3)

7	**Develop protocols and procedures for conducting coaching.**	• Who will be involved in setting out the ground rules for coaching in your school?
		• Do your protocols and procedures include:
		  – a code of conduct for coaching that includes a clear statement about confidentiality?
		  – mechanisms for establishing coaching partnerships and for dissolving them when the work is completed, or if the process is found to be of no benefit?
		  – clarity about the use of time for coaching?
		  – a method for evaluating the impact of coaching?
		(See Chapters 3, 8, and 9)

8	**Establish working coaching partnerships.**	• Will all staff be expected to engage in a coaching relationship?

(Continued)

	Steps to take	Questions to consider
9	Set up a forum for the discussion of issues arising from the coaching process.	• How will coaching partnerships be established? How will personalities and needs be matched? (See Chapter 9) • Will the forum be for all staff or for a group of identified coaches? • Who will chair the meetings? • How will confidentiality be maintained? (See Chapter 9)
10	Evaluate the impact of coaching on pedagogy and practice.	• How should coaches, coachees, children and colleagues with a monitoring role contribute to the evaluation of the impact of coaching in the school? • How will confidentiality be maintained when evaluating the success of the programme? (See Chapter 10)
11	Review the development and impact of coaching in the school and consider the steps for year 2.	• Have the targets been met? • In the second year, will coaching have a different focus? • Who will lead the second year of development? (See Chapters 4–7 for ideas about different uses and contexts for coaching)
12	Write the action plan for year 2.	• See step 2.

GLOSSARY

Active listening: Occurs when the coach pays full attention to the coachee's language, tone of voice, verbal images and figures of speech without being distracted by his or her own thoughts or internal listening.

Clarifying questions: Help the coachee to identify the issue with precision and to deepen thinking as well as to sort out misconceptions.

Coaching: A non-directive helping process that enables people to identify and clarify issues, solve problems, commit to action, develop their skills, motivation and self-esteem. The coach enables the coachee to find his or her own solutions by using the skills of listening, questioning, reflecting and clarifying.

Co-coaching: An activity in which two colleagues coach each other in order to develop aspects of their practice.

Group coaching: When one or two teachers coach a group of colleagues who may have similar issues.

Incisive questions: Questions that are intended to get to the nub of an issue and to cut through perceived limitations. They may present the coachee with real challenge. They should therefore be used with care.

Internal listening: The self-talk that goes on inside one's head that can act as 'interference' in a coaching conversation.

Intuitive listening: This occurs when the coach tunes in to the coachee's thoughts and feelings, to what is implied or suggested by non-verbal cues, to what lies under the surface of the conversation.

Leadership coaching: Coaching that focuses specifically on leadership issues.

Locus of control: The mechanisms that people perceive are present to guide and control the events in their lives and their behaviours. These may be *internal* (determined by self) or *external* (determined by others). In coaching, the aim is to help the coachee to identify which aspects of the situation are truly within their control.

Mentoring: A helping process in which the mentor will offer expert knowledge, advice and guidance. While the mentor may use the skills of coaching (listening, questioning, reflecting and clarifying), they have a responsibility to oversee colleagues and for the evaluation of progress.

Mirroring: Used by the coach to reflect the body posture of the coachee in order to put them at ease. This will require the coach to observe small signs in the body language of the colleague and to respond appropriately. It may involve, for example, adopting a similar seating position or respecting the coachee's sense of what constitutes a safe distance between the two individuals.

Outcome questions: Useful towards the end of the conversation when the coachee wishes to commit to action.

Peer coaching: A term used to stress that coaching is a relationship of equals.

Preferred future state: An imagined future in which issues are resolved. Coaches often help their clients to visualise this state in order to begin to formulate the first steps towards it.

Reflective questions: Help coachees to think about their practice and why they behave as they do as well as how they might change.

Scaling: A tool used in coaching to test the degree of success so far or to check commitment to future action. The coach may ask the coachee to assess, for example on a scale of one to ten, the likelihood of taking the next step. A low score in this case is likely to indicate lack of commitment or uncertainty about the course of action.

Self-talk (negative):   The state of mind in which we feel that we cannot control or improve our situation. The task of the coach is to assist the coachee to adopt realistic, positive self-talk rather than the action-sapping negative.

Self-talk (positive):   The talk that goes on in our heads in which we adopt a positive 'can do' attitude to our challenges.

Solution-focused coaching: A term used in the literature to stress the positive, action-focused nature of coaching – that it is concerned to assist the coachee to work *away from* a problem and *towards* a solution.

Specialist coaching: This occurs when a teacher uses specific expertise to support the development of a particular aspect of a colleague's practice. It may require real restraint on the part of the coach in order to avoid telling the coachee what to do.

Summarising questions: Help to focus the conversation and to clarify what has been said.

Team coaching: This occurs when a department or other distinct team within the staff use coaching techniques to develop their practice.

References

Department for Education and Skills (2004) *Pedagogy and Practice: Teaching and Learning in Secondary Schools*: London: DfES.

Flaherty, J. (1999*) Coaching: Evoking Excellence in Others*. London: Butterworth-Heinemann.

Fleming, I. and Taylor, A. (1998) *The Coaching Pocketbook*. Alresford: Management Pocketbooks.

Harbour, M. (1996) 'Collaboration, Competition and Cross-phase Liaison: The North Lowestoft Schools Network', in D. Bridges and C. Husbands (eds) *Consorting and Collaborating in the Education Marketplace*. London: Falmer Press.

Hawkins, P. and Smith, N. (2006) *Coaching, Mentoring and Organizational Consultancy: Supervision and Development*. Maidenhead: Open University Press.

Jackson, P.Z. and McKergow, M. (2007) The Solutions Focus: Making Coaching and Change SIMPLE (2nd edn). London: Nicholas Brealey Publishing.

Joyce, B. and Showers, B. (1996) 'The Evolution of Peer Coaching', *Educational Leadership*, 53(6): 12–16.

Joyce, B. and Showers, B. (2002) *Designing Training and Peer Coaching: Our Need for Learning*. Alexandria, VA: Association for Supervision and Curriculum Development.

Kelly, S. (2007) *The CPD Coordinator's Toolkit*. London: Paul Chapman Publishing.

Knowles, M., Holton, E. and Swanson, R. (2005) *The Adult Learner*. Boston, MA: Butterworth-Heinemann

Powell, G., Chambers, M. and Baxter, G. (2001) *Pathways to Coaching*. Bristol: TLO.

Rewards and Incentives Group (2007) *Performance Management for Teachers and Head Teachers – Guidance*. London: DfES.

Rotter, J.B. (1954) *Social Learning and Clinical Psychology*. Englewood Cliffs, NJ:

Starr, J. (2003) *The Coaching Manual*. London: Prentice Hall Business.

Thomas, W. (2005) *Coaching Solutions: Resource Book*. Stafford: Network Educational Press.

Thomas, W. and Smith, A. (2004) *Coaching Solutions: Practical Ways to Improve Performance in Education*. Stafford: Network Educational Press.

Whitmore, J. (2002) *Coaching for Performance*. London: Nicholas Brealey Publishing.

Index

Added to a page number 'f' denotes a figure.

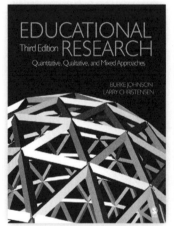

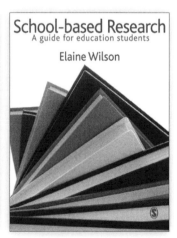

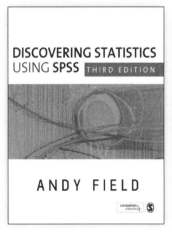
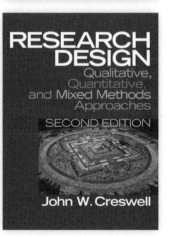